OSPREY COMBAT AIRCᴋᴀFT • 9

MOSQUITO
FIGHTER/FIGHTER-BOMBER
UNITS OF WORLD WAR 2

SERIES EDITOR: TONY HOLMES

OSPREY COMBAT AIRCRAFT • 9

MOSQUITO
FIGHTER/FIGHTER-BOMBER
UNITS OF WORLD WAR 2

Martin Bowman

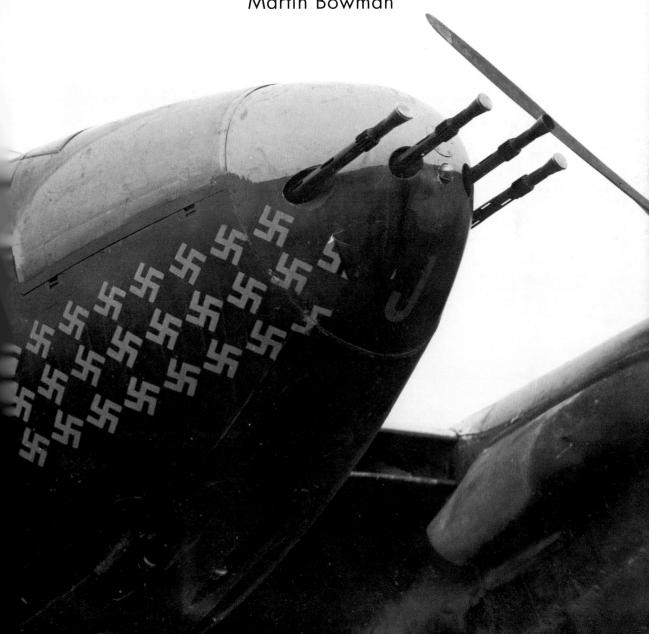

Front Cover
Trailing smoke and flame from its ruptured port wing tank inboard of the BMW 132T-2 radial engine, a Ju 52/3mg6e 'minesweeper' of the *Minensuchgruppe* descends towards a grey, watery grave in the Kattegat (the stretch of water that separates eastern Denmark from Sweden) off Sjaelland's Point. Fitted with a distinctive dural degaussing hoop for anti-mine work, this venerable Junkers transport was one of two downed on 14 April 1944 by marauding No 418 'City of Edmonton' Sqn Mosquito FB VI NS850, flown by Flt Lt Robert Kipp and navigator Flt Lt Peter Huletsky. The aircraft was on an ultra long-range 'Day Ranger' sortie across occupied Europe from its base at Holmesley South, in Dorset. The crew was also credited with destroying two Do 217s on the ground and damaging a third during the course of the same sortie, bringing their total of air-to-air victories thus far in the war to four and a half, plus one shared and a half 'probable'. Robert Kipp was awarded the DFC in May 1944, followed by a DSO two months later, while Peter Huletsky was awarded a DFC and Bar. Kipp finished the war with ten aircraft shot down, one shared destroyed, one shared probable, one damaged and seven destroyed and eight damaged on the ground. He left the RCAF in October 1945 but rejoined in 1946, only to be killed in a flying accident in a RCAF Vampire at St Hubert on 25 July 1949
(*cover artwork by Iain Wyllie*)

First published in Great Britain in 1998 by Osprey Publishing
Elms Court, Chapel Way, Botley, Oxford, OX2 9LP

ISBN 1 85532 731 7

Edited by Tony Holmes
Page design by TT Designs, T & B Truscott
Cover Artwork by Iain Wyllie
Aircraft Profiles by Chris Davey
Figure Artwork by Mike Chappell
Scale Drawings by Mark Styling

Origination by Valhaven Ltd, Isleworth
Printed in Hong Kong

99 00 01 02   10 9 8 7 6 5 4 3 2

ACKNOWLEDGEMENTS
The author wishes to thank the following individuals for their valued assistance during the compilation of this volume: Eric Atkins DFC* KW*, RAF Retd, Chairman, Mosquito Aircrew Assoc; Mrs Molly Baker; Dr Theo Boiten; Mike Bailey; Philip Birtles; Hank Cooper DSO DFC, RAF Retd; Tom Cushing; Sqn Ldr Dick Doleman RAF Retd; Stephen M Fochuk; Bernard Job RAF Retd; the late A Paul Mellows RAF Retd; Sqn Ldr R C 'Bob' Muir DFC, RAF Retd; Dick O'Farrell RAF Retd; Walter Rowley RAF Retd; Mrs Edna Scholefield; Jerry Scutts; Graham M Simons; Andy Thomas; Geoff Thomas; the late Leslie Turner RAF Retd; Brian Whitlock Blundell RAF Retd; and the late Tim Woodman RAF Retd.

EDITOR'S NOTE
To make this best-selling series as authoritative as possible, the editor would be extremely interested in hearing from any individual who may have relevant photographs, documentation or first-hand experiences relating to the elite pilots, and their aircraft, of the various theatres of war. Any material used will be fully credited to its original source. Please write to Tony Holmes at 10 Prospect Road, Sevenoaks, Kent, TN13 3UA, Great Britain.

CONTENTS

DEFENSIVE NIGHTFIGHTING

As the Mosquito nightfighter prototype, W4052 became only the second of de Havilland's 'wooden wonders' to take to the skies when it completed its maiden flight on 15 May 1941. The bomber version had flown on 25 November 1940, while photo-recce (PR) optimised W4051 completed the trio of flying prototypes when it completed its first flight on 10 June 1941 (see *Osprey Combat Aircraft 13 - Mosquito Photo-Reconnaissance Units of World War 2* for further details). The fighter version was armed with four 20 mm Hispano cannon and four .303-in Browning machine guns in a modified 'fighter nose'. Aside from being armed, the aircraft also differed from the bomber prototype through its use of two Rolls-Royce Merlin 21, 22 or 23 engines, each capable of producing 1460 hp (the bomber initially used just the Merlin 21), fitment of a flat bullet-proof windscreen, and the installation of the then ultra-secret AI (Air Intercept) Mk IV radar. Entry was through a door in the starboard side of the cockpit instead of through a trapdoor in the floor as on the bomber version. The aircraft also had strengthened wing spars to allow it to withstand the rigours of fighter combat. W4052, which was built to Specification F 21/40, was completed at Salisbury Hall and flown out of a field adjacent to the assembly hangar at Hatfield on 15 May 1941 by Geoffrey de Havilland Jr. There were the usual teething troubles associated with a new aircraft, especially with armament and the exhaust system. Flash eliminators were later fitted to the machine guns on the NF II to prevent the crew being blinded when they were fired at night.

Fighter prototype W4052 was constructed at Salisbury Hall and flown out of a field adjacent to the assembly hangar on 15 May 1941 by Geoffrey de Havilland Jr. After being used to test various armament modifications, W4052 joined the FIU at Ford and was eventually scrapped on 28 January 1946 (*DH*)

This view of NF II DD750 of No 157 Sqn reveals the aircraft's distinctive AI Mk IV 'arrowhead' nose- and wing-mounted azimuth aerials. This unit was the first in Fighter Command to operate the Mosquito nightfighter variant, and by mid-April 1942 some 20 aircraft had arrived. The first Mosquito sorties were flown on the night of 27/28 April, when three radar-equipped NF IIs tried to intercept raiders attacking Norwich. DD750 later served with Nos 25 and 264 Sqns before joining No 239 Sqn, within No 100 Group Bomber Support, on 11 December 1943 (*via Philip Birtles*)

NF II W4087 RS-B of No 157 Sqn is seen at Castle Camps in 1942. The all-black matt scheme could slow the aircraft by up to 23 mph (*Brian Whitlock Blundell Collection*)

On 21 June 1941 the Air Ministry ordered five prototype Mosquitoes (one bomber, one PR and three fighters), 19 PR models and 176 fighters. No 157 Sqn, which reformed at Debden, in Essex, on 3 December 1941 under the leadership of Wg Cdr Gordon Slade, became the first to operate the Mosquito nightfighter. On 17 January 1942, the unit took delivery of its first T III trainer, by which time it had moved north to Castle Camps, in Cambridgeshire, to begin working up on the new fighter.

Deliveries of Mosquitoes were slow, and only 14 NF IIs had arrived by the end of March 1942. Six more arrived in mid-April, although three of these were not fitted with complete AI radar sets, and only seven crews had been trained to fly the aircraft up to this point. The situation was the same at Wittering, where No 151 Sqn, led by Wg Cdr Irving Stanley Smith DFC, RNZAF, was re-equipping with NF IIs after having operated firstly Defiants, then Turbinlight Havocs. 'A' Flight had received DD608 on 6 April, but for the time being 'B' Flight would have to wait.

The need for radar-equipped nightfighters had become a matter of great urgency in the wake of the Luftwaffe commencing its series of *Baedeker* raids against British cities of historic or aesthetic importance. Hitler had ordered the terror raids as retribution for an attack by Bomber

Command on the historic city of Lübeck on 28/29 March 1942 – Exeter and Bath were the first British cities to suffer, and loss of life was heavy. At last, on 27/28 April No 157 Sqn flew its first Mosquito sorties, when three AI Mk V radar-equipped NF IIs joined 19 Beaufighters and Spitfires trying to intercept the *Baedeker* raid on Norwich, while KG 30 laid mines off the Norfolk coast. Radar contacts were made but none of the raiders could be intercepted, and the NF IIs developed various snags, not least cannon flash, exhaust manifold and cowling burning problems.

The following night the Luftwaffe bombed York, whilst 24 hours later Flt Lt Pennington in DD613 flew the first No 151 Sqn Mosquito sortie from Wittering when about 75 aircraft raided Britain. A Do 217 was chased by a No 157 Sqn NF II, but the Mosquito was spotted in the moonlight and contact lost. Meanwhile, the *Baedeker* raids continued.

On 3/4 May Exeter was bombed again, and on 4/5 May Cowes, on the Isle of Wight, was attacked. Then it was the turn of Norwich again on 8/9 May, followed by Hull and later Poole. The Mosquitoes had proven ineffective, failing to shoot down any of the attackers, and on 19 May, in the first of three NF II accidents that month, a No 157 Sqn aircraft suffered an engine failure and crashed at Castle Camps, killing both crewmen.

Finally, on 29/30 May during the Luftwaffe raid on Grimsby, the Mosquitoes at last found their mark. Firstly, No 151 Sqn's Flt Lt Pennington shot up a Do 217E-4, although his aircraft was hit by return fire during his second attack and his radar operator lost contact before the pilot could finish the enemy off. Pennington flew 140 miles back to Wittering on one engine. Meanwhile, way out over the North Sea squadronmates Plt Off John Wain and Flt Sgt Thomas S G Grieve in DD608 also succeeded in damaging a Do 217E-4 (from KG 2), whilst much farther south Sqn Ldr G Ashfield of No 157 Sqn scored a Do 217E-4 probable off Dover.

The following month saw Colerne-based No 264 Sqn fly their first operational Mosquito sorties (on the 13th) since starting conversion from the Defiant on 3 May. On 24/25 June the Luftwaffe mounted an unsuccessful raid on Nuneaton, with five bombers being claimed destroyed by

NF II HJ911 is seen fitted with early AI radar equipment. This aircraft was the first in a batch of 34 NF IIs delivered to the RAF from de Havilland's Leavesden plant between September and December 1942, HJ911 seeing service with Nos 157, 307 and 141 Sqns, before ending up with No 1692 Flt. It was eventually struck off charge on 19 February 1945 (*via Philip Birtles*)

British defences. One of these was credited to Wg Cdr Smith and his navigator, Flt Lt Kernon-Sheppard, in W4097, who intercepted three enemy aircraft during a hectic 30-minute period. At 2330 an He 111 was detected at 8000 ft, Smith closing to 300 yards before opening fire, but the Heinkel dived away trailing fuel from its port tanks as a second approach was made. An He 111H-6 of Erprp.u.Lehr. Kdo 17 (a testing unit) was badly damaged by a Mosquito when flares on board exploded. Bordfunker (radio-operator) Oberfeldwebel Paul Wilhelm Krause, baled out, prematurely as it turned out, because the Heinkel limped back to Holland and landed safely. Krause's body was washed ashore at Pakefield on 5 July. Ten minutes later, Smith was vectored on to Do 217E-4 F8+AC of II./KG 40. This time he approached unseen to 100 yards before opening fire, causing the bomber to dive into the sea and explode.

At 2348 radar contact was made with another Do 217E-4 (U5+AB of I./KG 2, flown by Leutnant Karl von Manowarda), and Smith closed and opened fire from 200 yards. Both the bomber's wing tanks exploded and the aircraft was engulfed in flames. The Kiwi pilot closed still further and fired a short burst to finish it off, U5+AB crashing into The Wash.

The following night, Plt Off Wain and Flt Sgt Grieve forced a He 111H-6 down into the North Sea in DD616 (this crew failed to return in DD623 on 10/11 August), and on 26/27 June Flt Lt Moody and Plt Off Marsh (again from No 151 Sqn) destroyed a Do 217E-4 of 3./KG 2, flown by Feldwebel Hans Schrödel, when Norwich was bombed again.

That elusive confirmed first kill for No 157 Sqn did not come with the arrival of the new month, although on the 27/28th Sqn Ldr Ashfield claimed a He 111 destroyed over the North Sea – No 151 Sqn, meanwhile, were credited with the destruction of four Dorniers that month.

The first of these had come on 21/22 July when Plt Off Fisher, in W4090, shot down Oberfeldwebel Heinrich Wolpers and his crew in 7./KG 2 Do 217E-4 U5+IH off Spurn Head. On 27/28 July two more Dorniers, flown by Feldwebel Richard Stumpf of I./KG 2, and Leutnant Hans-Joachim Mohring of 3./KG 2, were downed by Plt Off E A Field-

This AI-equipped NF II (DD737) was one of the first Mosquitoes issued to No 85 Sqn when it converted to the de Havilland nightfighter from the Havoc at Hunsdon in August 1942. DD737 was delivered to No 30 MU (Maintenance Unit) on 29 August 1942, and then to No 85 Sqn on 21 September. It was passed to No 264 Sqn on 13 March 1943, and then returned 'to the works' on 6 May. After languishing in various MUs, it joined the Bomber Support Development Unit (BSDU) on 14 October 1944, before passing to No 54 Operational Training Unit (OTU) at Acklington, with whom it was lost on 6 December 1944 when it failed to return from a cross-country exercise

Wg Cdr Gordon Slade (right), OC No 157 Sqn, with his adjutant (left) and engineering officer (centre) at Castle Camps in 1942. Slade had joined the RAF in 1933, and four years later began a career as a test pilot at the A&AEE (Aircraft & Armaments Experimental Establishment) at Martlesham Heath. In September 1941 he was promoted to wing commander and attached to No 604 Sqn at Middle Wallop, where he learned the art of nightfighting under the expert tutelage of John Cunningham, before taking command of No 157 Sqn in December 1941. On 22/23 August 1942 Slade and his radar operator, Plt Off Philip Truscott, destroyed Do 217E-4 U5+LP of 6./KG 2, flown by Deputy _Staffelkapitan_ Oberleutnant Hans Walter Wolff, over Worlingworth. By October 1944 Slade had taken command of No 169 Sqn, and in April 1945 he was promoted to group captain. After the war he resumed his career as an RAF test pilot, before joining the Fairey Group in 1965. He died in October 1981
(_Brian Whitlock Blundell Collection_)

ing and now Sqn Ldr Pennington. Finally, on 29/ 30 July, Flg Off A I McRitchie destroyed Do 217E-4 U5+GV (flown by Oberfeldwebel Artur Hartwig) of II./KG2 during a raid on Birmingham.

The sole Mosquito claim for August came on the 22nd/23rd when No 157 Sqn scored its first confirmed kill. Patrolling from Castle Camps, OC, Wg Cdr Gordon Slade, accompanied by Plt Off P V Truscott, destroyed Do 217E-4 U5+LP of 6./KG 2, flown by Oberleutnant Hans Walter Wolff, Deputy _Staffelkapitän_ and an ex-Lufthansa pilot.

However, following its initial success, No 157 Sqn endured a lean September. On the 7th Plt Off G Deakin damaged a Do 217 over Hunsdon, whilst on the 30th Wg Cdr R F H Clerke destroyed a Ju 88A-4 off the Dutch coast – this was No 157 Sqn's first day combat victory of the war.

Not to be outdone, No 151 Sqn notched two confirmed kills (both Do 217E-4s). The first fell near Orwell, in Cambridgeshire, on 8/9 September during a raid on Bedford, Flg Off Ian McRitchie and Flt Sgt E S James using DD669 to down F8+AP (on loan to 3./KG 2), piloted by Feldwebel Alfred Witting. The second came on the 17th/18th during a raid on King's Lynn when Flt Lt H E Bodien DFC and Sgt G B Brooker (in DD610) destroyed U5+UR of 7./KG 2, piloted by Feldwebel Franz Elias. On 26 October No 157 Sqn scored the last NF II kill of 1942 when Flg Off E H Cave (in DD716) downed a Ju 88D-1 off Beachy Head.

Successes in the early months of 1943 were few and far between. On 15/16 January Flt Sgt E A Knight, RCAF and Sgt W I L Roberts of No 151 Sqn used DD609 to down Do 217E-4 U5+KR of 7./KG 2, piloted by Leutnant Günther Wolf, during a raid on Lincoln. The Dornier crashed at Boothby Graffoe Coleby, in Lincolnshire, killing all aboard.

On 17/18 January No 85 Sqn – one of the RAF's most famous fighter units, with the appropriate motto _Noctu diuque venamur_ ('We hunt by day and night') – notched its first victory since converting from Havocs to NF IIs at Hunsdon in August 1942. Appropriately, it fell to unit OC, Wg Cdr G L Raphael DFC*, who, along with Wt Off Addison DFM, destroyed a Ju 88A-14 from I./KG 6 (an experienced Pathfinder unit).

On 22 January Flt Sgt B M Haight of No 410 'Cougar' Sqn RCAF, used HJ929 to destroy a Do 217E east of Hartlepool. Mosquito units now had to wait until March before the 'killing season' began again.

It was not until 18/19 March that the nightfighters once more tasted success, opposing bombers sent to attack Norwich and Great Yarmouth encountering appreciable numbers of both Mosquitoes and Beaufighters. Flg Off Deakin (with Plt Off de Costa) added a kill to his damaged claim of September 1942 in W4099 when he was credited with a Ju 88A-14 destroyed off Harwich, whilst Flg Off D Williams and Plt Off P Dalton of No 410 Sqn used HK936 to down Do 217E-4 Wk-Nr 5523 U5+AH of 1./KG 2, flown by Unteroffizier Horst Toifel. The latter tried desperately to elude the Mosquito by carrying out a half roll and diving for the ground, but Williams followed him. At 1800 ft the Mosquito pilot pulled out of his dive but Toifel and his crew did not pull out of theirs. The Do 217 exploded near Terrington St Clements, killing all onboard.

On 28/29 March 47 bombers of _IX. Fliegerkorps_ again bombed Norwich, and once more the nightfighters tasted success. One crew embroiled in the action was No 157 Sqn's Flg Off John R Beckett, RAAF, and Flt Sgt Phillips, who took off from Bradwell Bay in W4079 to patrol

an area some 30 miles off Orfordness. Once on station, they were vectored by HCI Trimley Heath on to a 'bogey' approaching Lowestoft and after two momentary contacts, Phillips obtained another contact dead ahead flying west at 12,000ft. It was changing course and height as it approached the coast, and after some difficulty, Beckett closed to 1000 ft to obtain a 'visual' of the target. The aircraft was Do 217E-4 U5+NM Wk-Nr 4375 of IV./KG 2, flown by Feldwebel Paul Huth.

Searchlights and anti-aircraft defences made identification difficult for the Mosquito crew, and they took several hits. As Beckett closed, the Dornier's rear gunner 'opened up' at them but missed, and the Australian returned fire immediately with two two-second bursts of cannon fire from a distance of 400 ft. Sparks flew off the Do 217 as hits were recorded, the bomber diving into cloud and crashing into the sea off Horsey, north of Great Yarmouth – Huth and his crew were killed. Beckett and Phillips' victory was shared with a Czech Beaufighter crew from No 68 Sqn.

Four aircraft were downed by Mosquitoes during April, three of them falling to No 85 Sqn, which had re-equipped with the NF XII. Just 97 NF XIIs were built, all of which were conversions from the NF II. Powered by 1460-hp Merlin 21s or 23s, and armed with four 20 mm cannon, the aircraft's main distinguishing feature was its 'thimble-nose' housing a powerful transmitter with a parabolic reflector for the 10 cm-wavelength AI Mk VIII radar, which removed the need for any external aerials.

No 85 Sqn's first NF XII victories came on 14/15 April when Sqn Ldr Peter Green and Flt Sgt A R Grimstone destroyed Do 217E-4 F8+AM from 4./KG 40 during a raid on Chelmsford, and Flt Lt Geoff Howitt and Flg Off George Irving claimed a Do 217-E-4 (U5+DP of 6./KG 2, flown by Unteroffizier Franz Tannenberger) off Clacton.

That same night south-west of Colchester, No 157 Sqn's Flt Lt James Gilles Benson DFC and Flt Lt Lewis Brandon DSO, DFC used NF II DD730 to shoot down a second 6./KG 2 Do 217E-4 (U5+KP, flown by Unteroffizier Walter Schmurr), the Dornier crashing at Layer Breton Heath, south-west of Colchester. Schmurr, observer Leutnant Karl-

No 85 Sqn pilots and navigators pose in front of a newly-delivered Mosquito NF XII at RAF Hunsdon in the spring of 1943. On the night of 21/22 March, Flt Lt Edward Nigel Bunting (sixth from left in the front row), with his navigator, Flt Lt C P Reed DFC (fifth from left, front row), shot down two aircraft in a single sortie whilst temporarily flying from Bradwell Bay, in Essex. Bunting was one of the pilots who operationally tested the high-altitude Mk XV, reaching a record altitude of 44,600 ft on 30 March 1943. On 13/14 July 1943 Bunting and his navigator, Freddie French, scored the first Me 410 kill for the nightfighter force when they shot down 16./KG 2 A-1 U5+KG (flown by Feldwebel Franz Zwiler and Oberfeldwebel Leo Raida) into the sea off Felixstowe. Bunting added a bar to his DFC and had scored nine confirmed victories by the time he was shot down and killed by flak on 30/31 July 1944 while chasing a radar contact over France (*Andrew Long*)

Heinrich Hertam and gunner Unteroffizier Martin Schwarz baled out, although radio operator/gunner Unteroffizier Franz Witte was found dead in the wreckage. On 24/25 April Flg Off J P M Lintott and Sgt G G Gilling-Lax of No 85 Sqn fired at Ju 88A-14 3E+HS of 8./KG 6 and it disintegrated in mid-air, the wreckage falling onto the streets of Bromley.

May brought more successes, with Plt Off R L Watts and Sgt J Whewell of No 157 Sqn downing a Do 217E-4 ten miles north-east of Colchester on the 13th/14th. The increased levels of action that the Mosquito was now experiencing proved that the aircraft was becoming a severe obstacle to German night bombing operations over England. The Germans responded by introducing Focke-Wulf Fw 190A-4/U8s of *Schnelles Kampfgeschwader* (SKG) 10 into the action, these nuisance raiders carrying a single 250-kg or 500-kg bomb on a centreline rack. This in turn, prompted Fighter Command to move Nos 85 and 157 Sqns from Hunsdon to West Malling and from Bradwell to Hunsdon respectively on 13 May so that they could better counter the threat posed by the fighter-bombers from France. The Mosquito crews found to their great joy and satisfaction that by using maximum continuous power from the Merlins throughout the whole climb from take-off to interception, combined with skillful use of the radar, it was just possible to intercept and close in, identify and then shoot down an Fw 190A-4/U8 carrying a bomb.

When, on the night of 16/17 May the Fw 190A-4/U8s of I./SKG10 flew in low and fast over the Straits of Dover, they were met in strength by No 85 Sqn, and four (possibly five) of the enemy fighter-bombers were shot down. Sqn Ldr Peter Green and Flt Sgt A R Grimstone were the first Mosquito crew to down an SKG 10 aircraft over Britain when they destroyed an Fw 190A-4/U8 near Dover, whilst Flt Lt Geoff Howitt and Flg Off G Irving 'bagged' a second 15 miles south of Hastings. A third Fw 190 fell to the guns of Flg Off Bernard J Thwaites and Plt Off Bill Clemo over the Straits of Dover after they had chased an aircraft all the way to the French coast before being recalled to West Malling. In mid-Channel Clemo picked up a free-lance contact crossing in front of them, and Thwaites shot it down from 50 yards astern. Despite their NF XII being hit by debris from the exploding fighter, Thwaites managed to score three hits on a second Fw 190 to claim it as a 'probable'. Finally, Flg Off J D

The crew of NF II DZ716/UP-L of No 605 'County of Warwick' Sqn prepare to fire up the aircraft's Merlins prior to setting off on a dusk sortie from Castle Camps in May 1943. This aircraft only enjoyed the briefest of frontline careers, for it stalled and crashed whilst attempting to land at the Cambridgeshire airfield on 7 July 1943 (*via Philip Birtles*)

Shaw and Plt Off A C Lowton braved their own searchlights to down the fourth Fw 190A-4/U8 of the night off Gravesend, returning to base with their windscreen coated in soot and their rudder badly damaged.

There was now no stopping No 85 Sqn. On 19/20 May Lintott and Gilling-Lax downed an Fw 190A-5 of 2./SKG 10, and on the 21st/22nd another Fw 190A was destroyed when Sqn Ldr Edward Crew DFC* and Flg Off Freddie French shot down a fighter into the sea 25 miles north-west of Hardelot. Finally, on 29/30 May Lintott and Gilling-Lax destroyed Ju 88S-1 3Z+SZ of I./KG 66, this aircraft being the first of the very fast Junkers 'twins' to fall on English soil. The Ju 88S-1 not only boasted power-boosted BMW 801G-2 engines fitted with the GM-1 nitrous-oxide injection system, but was also stripped of its ventral gondola – defensive armament comprised just one MG 131 machine-gun. As a result of these modifications, the S-1 was difficult to overhaul and Lintott had to climb to 29,000 ft in stages before he finally saw his prey. One of the three high-pressure nitrous-oxide storage tanks aft of the bomb bay was duly struck by his fire, and the Ju 88S-1 exploded into tiny fragments.

During June more Mosquito squadrons got in on the act of destroying enemy bombers over Britain and over the North Sea and Channel approaches. On 5 June a No 29 Sqn NF XII destroyed a Ju 88-A14 off Ostend, and on the 11th another NF XII from No 256 Sqn, piloted by

Wg Cdr John Cunningham DSO* DFC* admires the new No 85 Sqn crest held up by Squadron Intelligence Officer, Flg Off E A Robertson, at Hunsdon on 5 May 1943. Cunningham, who obtained 16 victories with Flt Lt Jimmy Rawnsley DFC whilst flying Beaufighters between November 1940 and May 1942, changed to the Mosquito NF XII in the summer of 1943. The pair scored their first victory with the new type flying DZ302/R on 13/14 June 1943 when they downed Fw 190A-5 CO+LT, flown by Leutnant Ullrich of 3./SKG 10 – the aircraft crashed at Nettlefold Farm, Borough Green, near Wrotham in Kent. They destroyed two more Fw 190s in this Mosquito on 23/24 August and 8/9 September. In 1944 Cunningham and Rawnsley destroyed a Me 410 on 2/3 January, claimed a Ju 188 as damaged on 20/21 February and finished their wartime scoring with a Ju 88 probable on 23/24 February. Cunningham's total stood at twenty aircraft destroyed, three probables and seven damaged by war's end

No 85 Sqn's Sqn Ldr Wilfrith Peter Green, OC 'A' Flight, Wg Cdr John Cunningham, squadron OC, and Sqn Ldr Edward Crew DFC*, OC 'B' Flight, pose at Hunsdon on 5 May 1943. Green achieved three kills before being posted to No 410 Sqn in March 1944 – on 14/15 April 1943 he and Flt Sgt A R Grimstone destroyed a Do 217E-4 over Clacton-on-Sea, followed on 16/17 May with an Fw 190A-4/U8 off Dover. Soon after this success Green was awarded the DFC (a DSO followed in 1944) and Grimstone the DFM. Finally, on 26/27 July they claimed a Ju 88 near Ramsgate. John Green went on to destroy a further 11 aircraft and 13 V1s whilst flying with Nos 410, 96 and 219 Sqns (he was OC of the latter unit from 11 August 1944 through to March 1945). Edward Crew had downed eight aircraft flying Blenheims and Beaufighters with No 604 Sqn before gaining his first NF II kill on 21/22 May 1942 when he and Flg Off Freddy French 'bagged' an Fw 190A near Hardelot. Green destroyed three more aircraft with No 96 Sqn (he was OC from June 1943 to 12 December 1944) and 21 V1s, to take his final score to 12 and 1 shared destroyed, and five damaged

Flg Off Burnett, downed a Do 217 south of Ford. That same day Flt Lt Joe Singleton and Flg Off W G Haslam of No 25 Sqn destroyed a Ju 88 on an 'Instep' patrol over the Bay of Biscay. On the night of 13/14 June, OC No 85 Sqn, 16-kill Beaufighter ace Wg Cdr John Cunningham DSO* DFC*, and Flt Lt C F 'Jimmy' Rawnsley DFC DFM*, used DZ302 to chase Fw 190-A5 CO+LT of 3./SKG 10 over their station at West Malling. Cunningham fired and the Fw 190 reared straight up on its nose, flicked over and plunged straight down, crashing at Borough Green, near Wrotham. Incredibly, the pilot was catapulted through the canopy and made a PoW. It was Cunningham's first Mosquito kill.

The following night, whilst flying NF XVII HK315, Flt Lts M J Gloster DFC and J F Oswold DFC of No 219 Sqn downed a Ju 88 in the Harwich area. Two nights later, Lt Johan Rød (a Norwegian pilot serving with No 85 Sqn) claimed an Fw 190 'probable' in an NF XII, whilst on 19 June Flt Lt H E Bodien DFC of No 151 Sqn destroyed a Ju 88 over the Bay of Biscay. Victories for the month ended on 21/22 June with another Fw 190 being downed (this time GP+LA of 2./SKG 10) into the River Medway by Flt Lt Bill McGuire and Flg Off W D Jones of No 85 Sqn.

July saw an upsurge in Mosquito operations, and the first victory during the month falling to an FIU (fighter Interceptor Unit) crew at Ford on 2/3 July – Wg Cdr R A Chisholm DFC and Flg Off N L Bamford DFC used HK166 to destroy a Ju 88D-1 45 miles south of Bognor. On the 9th, Flg Off J P M Lintott and Sgt G G Gilling-Lax of No 85 Sqn destroyed Do 217K-1 U5+FP, piloted by Oberleutnant Hermann Zink of 6./KG 2, when they collided with the bomber. Zink and his crew crashed at Detling and were all killed, whilst Lintott and Gilling-Lax were found dead two miles away in the wreckage of their Mosquito.

On 11/12 July Sqn Ldr A G Lawrence DFC, RCAF and Flt Sgt H J Wilmer DFM of No 410 Sqn destroyed Do 217M-1 U5+EL of 3./KG 2, flown by Unteroffizier Willy Spielmanns, ten miles east of the mouth of the Humber in HJ944. Two nights later Flt Lt Edward Nigel Bunting and Flg Off Freddie French of No 85 Sqn downed the first Me 410 'Hornisse' ('Hornet') to be destroyed over Britain when they downed Me 410A-1 U5+KG, crewed by Feldwebel Franz Zwiler and Oberfeldwebel Leo Raida, of 16./KG 2 off Felixstowe. On the night of 15/16 July, Flt Lt B J Thwaites and Plt Off Bill Clemo, again from No 85 Sqn, destroyed a second Me 410A-1, (U5+OT of V./KG 2, flown by Hauptmann Friederich-Wilhelm

NF II DD739/RX-X of No 456 Sqn, RAAF is seen in June 1943 whilst on a training a flight from Middle Wallop, in Hampshire. An ex-No 85 Sqn aircraft, this Mosquito was lost on 3/4 December 1943 whilst on a high-level bomber support mission (known as a 'Mahmoud') to Kassel, in Germany. Plt Off Tommy May and Flg Off Les Parnell were both posted missing in action (*DH via Basil McCrea*)

Crews from No 456 Sqn, RAAF are seen at Colerne just prior to manning up for a day sortie on 23 September 1943. They are, from left to right: Flg Off M N Austin; Wt Off A S McEvoy; Flg Off R S Williams; Flt Lt G Panitz; Plt Off G Gatenby; Flt Sgt A J Keating (kneeling); Plt Off J M Fraser; Flg Off J W Newell; Plt Off A M Abbey; and Flg Off S D P Smith (*RAAF*)

Methner and Unteroffizier Hubert Grube) whilst patrolling off Dunkirk.

Five more aircraft were destroyed by Mosquitoes before the month was out, one of these falling to a No 29 Sqn crew who downed a Ju 88 north-east of Foreness. On 18 July a No 256 Sqn NF XII crew 'bagged' an Fw 190 over the Channel, and on 25/26 July Flg Off Knowles of No 605 Sqn (flying an NF II) destroyed Do 217M-1 U5+KL, flown by Leutnant Manfred Lieddert of 3./KG 2, off Hull. The following night Sqn Ldr Peter Green DFC and Flt Sgt A R Grimstone DFM of No 85 Sqn claimed a Ju 88 east of Ramsgate, and on 29/30 July Wg Cdr G R Park, OC No 256 Sqn destroyed Me 410A-1 U5+BJ, crewed by Oberleutnant Helmut Biermann and Unteroffizier Willi Kroger, south of Beachy Head.

On 5/6 August No 604 'County of Middlesex' Sqn scored their first NF XIII victories since converting to the Mosquito from the Beaufighter at Scorton in April when Flt Lt J A M Haddon and Flg Off R J McIlvenny downed a Ju188 and a Ju88 over Rennes in MM514. The NF XIII had a universal wing similar to that fitted to the FB VI bomber, and boasted AI Mk VIII radar in a 'thimble', or Universal, ('bull') nose. On 15/16 August the Luftwaffe lost seven aircraft over Britain and France, Wg Cdr Park opening No 85 Sqn's scoring for the month with a double Do 217M-1 haul. The first was flown by Unteroffizier Karl Morgenstern, whilst the second had Unteroffizier Franz Bündgens at the controls – both fell near Selsey. That same night No 410 Sqn's Plt Off Rayne D Schultz and Flg Off V A Williams used NF VI HP849 to down Do 217M-1 U5+GT of 9./KG 2, flown by Unteroffizier Josef Schultes, off Beachy Head.

On the night of 22/23 August Sqn Ldr Geoff Howitt DFC and Plt Off J C O Medworth of No 85 Sqn downed Me 410A-1 U5+AF of 15./KG 2 (crewed by Feldwebel Walter Hartmann and Obergefreiter Michael Meurer) at Chelmondiston, while a second No 85 Sqn crew destroyed an Fw 190 near Dunkirk. East of Manston, No 29 Sqn's Flt Lt C Kirkland

Wearing large leather gauntlets, Wg Cdr Vashon James 'Pop' Wheeler (he was born in 1898) DFC*, MC*, Order of St Stanislaus (Russia), was OC No 157 Sqn from 29 December 1942 through to August 1943. He is seen here at Bradwell Bay with his navigator, Flt Lt Borridge. 'Pop' Wheeler had seen active service during World War 1 as a second lieutenant in the Rifle Brigade between 1916-18, and in 1919 was part of the ill-fated British Expedition to Russia in support of Czarist forces opposing the communist revolution. Learning to fly during the 1920s, and duly becoming an airline pilot, Wheeler's multi-engine experience came in extremely handy when he was initially posted onto transport aircraft with the outbreak of war in Europe in September 1939. After completing a tour on Ansons, he flew a further 71 combat sorties on Hurricanes, Havocs and Beaufighters with No 85 Sqn – he claimed two enemy aircraft destroyed in early 1941 whilst with this unit. Wheeler completed a further 29 defensive patrols with No 157 Sqn, before flying the unit's first Intruder operation on 23 March 1943. On 26 February 1944 Wheeler took command of Lancaster-equipped No 207 Sqn, 'Pop' flying on every operation the unit undertook until he was killed in action on the night of 22/23 March 1944 on a sortie to Frankfurt. It was his 158th operational flight (*Brian Whitlock Blundell Collection*)

and Plt Off R C Raspin used NF XII HK197 to down an Me 410A-1, while two other crews from the same unit claimed two more 'Hornets'.

The following night Wg Cdr Cunningham and Flt Lt Rawnsley (in NF XII DZ302) destroyed a Fw 190 off Dunkirk, and 24 hours later No 85 Sqn struck again when Norwegians Capt Johan Rød and Capt Leif Lîvestad DFM* shared in the destruction of Me 410A-1 U5+DG of 16./KG 2 with Wg Cdr R E X Mack DFC of No 29 Sqn.

September was notable for more high-scoring from No 85 Sqn, who claimed six aircraft, including four Fw 190A-5s – Howitt and Irving got one, Cunningham and Rawnsley another and Thwaites and Clemo destroyed two. On the 15th/16th Flg Off Jarris of No 29 Sqn used NF XII HK189 to down 15./KG 2's Oberfeldwebel Horst Müller and Unteroffizier Wolfgang Dose in Me 410A-1 U5+AF off Beachy Head. That same night a 9./KG 2 Do 217M-1 (flown by Oberfeldwebel Erich Mosler) crashed into the sea off Ramsgate after being attacked by Flt Lt Watts of No 488 Sqn, whilst No 85 Sqn's Flg Off E R Hedgecoe and Plt Off Witham downed Ju 88A-14 3E+FP of 6./KG 6.

During October Mosquitoes of Nos 85, 488, 151 and 29 Sqns accounted for 16 enemy aircraft, 11 of which fell to the Wg Cdr Cunningham's unit. This total included No 85 Sqn's first Ju 188, which fell to Flg Off Holloway and Wt Off Stanton south-east of Dover on the 8th/9th, plus another victory for Sqn Ldr Thwaites and Plt Off Clemo. Flt Lt Edward Bunting scored his third victory on 8/9 October when he

No 157 Sqn's 'A' Flight pose for a formal group photograph at Predannack in December 1943. Flight Commander Sqn Ldr James G Benson can be seen smiling in the centre of the shot, while Brian Blundell is in the top row holding 'Dolly' Doleman's dog, 'Towser'. On Blundell's right are Flt Lts Brooks (Doleman's navigator), Hull (Blundell's navigator) and Huckin. The latter, and his navigator Edwards, ditched in the Bay of Biscay during their tour with this unit following combat. They quickly evacuated their sinking aircraft and got into their dinghy, before transferring to a life-boat dropped by an air-sea rescue Warwick. The pair then sailed to the Cornish port of Newlyn. Huckin and Edwards were subsequently decorated for their daring escape (*Brian Whitlock Blundell Collection*)

forced 7./KG 6 Ju 88S-1 3E+NR down into the sea ten miles south of Dover. This crew scored their second victory of the month on the 17th/18th, when Me 410 U5+LF of 15./KG 2 fell to their guns.

November saw the Luftwaffe lose a further eight aircraft to Mosquito nightfighters from Nos 29, 85, 410 and 488 Sqns, with one of the most remarkable kills falling to Flt Sgt Jaworski of No 307 'City of Lvov' Polish Sqn in NF II HJ651, who destroyed an Fw 200 Kondor 120 miles north-east of the Shetlands on the 22nd. Another No 307 Sqn crew claimed a Ju88D-1 on 9 December, whilst on the night of the 10th/11th, Flg Offs Rayne D Schultz and V A Williams of No 410 Sqn used NF II DZ292 to destroy three Do 217M-1s during a raid on Chelmsford.

Flt Lts Landrey and 'Steve' Stephens of No 157 Sqn pose atop their Mosquito at Hunsdon in 1943 (*Brian Whitlock Blundell Collection*)

'BABY BLITZ' AND BEYOND

In January 1944 crews from Nos 85, 488, 29, 96, 151 and 410 Sqns scored 15 confirmed kills (and two probables). Many of these fell to the 50 NF XIIIs within Fighter Command that had had their Merlin engines modified to use Nitrous Oxide (better known as 'laughing gas'), which mixed with petrol to give the aircraft added performance at altitude. Success with the 'new' Mosquito came early, as on the 2nd/3rd Wg Cdr Cunningham and Flt Lt Rawnsley used HK374 to down an Me 410 near Sandwich. On the night of 21/22 January 92 bombers, led by Pathfinders, headed for London and East Anglia loaded with incendiaries in the first of a series of revenge raids on Britain code-named Operation *Steinbock* (dubbed the 'Baby Blitz' by the RAF). *Düppel* ('Window') was scattered by the attacking force in an effort to confuse British radar.

This simple device did not save He 177A-5 Wk-Nr 15747 of I./KG 40, however, as it became the first Greif shot down over Britain when it fell to the guns of NF XII HK193 flown by Flg Off H K Kemp and Flt Sgt J R Maidment of No 151 Sqn. On patrol from Colerne, the Mosquito crew intercepted the bomber over Whitmore Vale, near Hindhead in Surrey. This Greif was just one of a dozen Luftwaffe aircraft downed by Mosquitoes during a raid which cost the Germans 21 bombers in total.

As more *Steinbock* raids, organised by 'Attack Leader England', Oberst Dietrich Peltz, followed from 28/29 January onwards, the toll of aircraft lost to Mosquito nightfighters steadily rose. On the night of 3/4 February 60 bombers were met by six squadrons of Mosquitoes, with Nos 85, 410 and 488 Sqns succeeding in downing four of the raiders. By the end of the month, Mosquitoes had destroyed a further 28 enemy aircraft during raids on Britain.

Steinbock continued into March over East Anglia and London, the raids being met with increasing ferocity and determination by Fighter Command. One of the most successful Mosquito crews during this period comprised Flt Lt Joe Singleton DFC and Flg Off Geoff Haslam of No 25 Sqn, at Coltishall. On 14/15 March they destroyed a Ju 188, which crashed into the sea off Southwold, whilst five nights later they shot down three Ju 88s in

Wg Cdr J A Mackie (left), OC No 157 Sqn from August 1943 through to March 1944, is seen with his navigator-radar operator, Flt Lt Scholfield
(*Brian Whitlock Blundell Collection*)

Sqn Ldr Herbert Tappin DFC and Flg Off I H Thomas, also of No 157 Sqn, are seen at Predannack in 1943. On 8/9 February 1944 they destroyed a Blohm und Voss Bv 222 Viking six-engined flying boat of 1.(F)/129 during a Night Ranger from Predannack to Biscarosse Lake, in France
(*Brian Whitlock Blundell Collection*)

Modified NF II DZ659/G was fitted with two Merlin 21s and an AI Mk X (US SCR.720/729 'Eleanora') radar in a universal nose fairing. The fighter served with the FIU throughout its service career (*DH via Basil McCrea*)

A Ju 290 burns atop the waves on 19 February 1944 after being shot down by a No 157 Sqn aircraft on an Instep patrol. The unit flew these challenging long-range day sweeps of the Western Approaches and the Bay of Biscay until April 1944 (*Richard Doleman*)

On the night of 24/25 February 1944 this Ju 88A-4 of 8./KG 6 was downed at Withyham, in Sussex, by Flt Lts R C Pargeter and R L Fell of No 29 Sqn in NF XIII HK422. The pair also destroyed a Ju 188 at Shorne, Kent, on the same night (*ARP*)

In total No 29 Sqn claimed six enemy aircraft shot down on 24/25 February 1944. This photo of 'A' Flight at Ford shows (back row, left to right); Flt Lt R L Fell, Flg Offs J E Barry, G Hopkins and Raspin, and Wt Off Nicol. Front Row (left to right); Wt Off Kershaw, Flt Lt Ted Cox (both Cox and Kershaw combined to destroy a He 177 on the 24/25 February some 30-35 miles south of Beachy Head at 2115 hours), Flg Off W W Provan, Sqn Ldr C Kirkland and Flt Lt R C Pargeter. Kirkland and Raspin destroyed a Do 217M at Dorking, in Surrey, on the 24th/25th, while Barry and Hopkins also downed a Dornier and claimed an Me 410 as a probable (*Ted Cox via Dr Theo Boiten*)

On 21/22 March 1944 No 410 Sqn's Flg Off S B Huppert and Plt Off J S Christie used HK456 to shoot down a Ju 88A-4 of 4/KG 30 over Latchingdon, in Essex. On 3 July 1944, Huppert (this time in MM570) destroyed a Ju 188 and an Me 410, before being shot down by defensive fire from the 'Hornisse' (*ARP*)

the space of just 13 minutes. Singleton, who was awarded the DSO, finished the war with seven kills.

Edward Bunting, now a squadron leader (and recipient of the DFC) with No 488 Sqn, and his navigator, Flt Lt C P Reed DFC, also tasted success during March with a trio of kills. On the night of the 14th/15th they used NF XIII MM476 to down a Ju 188 over Great Leighs, Essex, and this was followed exactly a week later with a double haul (again in MM476) – Bunting downed Ju 88A-4 4D+AT of 9./KG 30, flown by Oberfeldwebel Nikolaus Mayer, over Suffolk, the bomber crashing in flames at Blacklands Hall, Cavendish. Two of the crew baled out and were taken prisoner, but Mayer and another crewmember died in the crash.

Bunting and Reed were then vectored towards another 'bogey', which turned out to be Ju 188E-1 3E+BK of 2./KG 6, flown by Leutnant G Lahl. Bunting pursued his quarry through a series of tight turns and steep climbs before he got into his favoured astern position and repeatedly pumped short bursts into the Junkers bomber from 250 yards. Lahl's machine hit the ground and exploded near Butlers Farm at Shopland, in Essex. Four crew were killed and the sole survivor, who baled out, taken prisoner. Bunting, who latter added a bar to his DFC, had achieved nine confirmed kills by the time he was shot down and killed by flak on 30 July 1944 while chasing a radar contact over France.

Other notable victories scored during March included a double haul (a Do 217 and a He 177A-3) on the night of the 19th/20th by Flt Lt D H Greaves DFC and Flg Off F M Robbins DFC of No 25 Sqn in NF XVII HK278. Flt Sgt C J Vlotman and Sgt J L Wood of No 488 Sqn also got 'a pair' in NF XIII HK365 when they destroyed a Ju 188 and a Ju 88 on 21/22 March, while 48 hours later Flt Lt Bernard Thwaites and Flg Off Bill Clemo used an NF XII to down an Fw 190 off Hastings, thus bringing the former's score to five.

Flt Lt Joe Singleton DFC (left) and Flg Off Geoff Haslam of No 25 Sqn destroyed a Do 217 on 20/21 February 1944, followed by three Ju 88s/188s in the space of 13 minutes on 19/20 March (*the late Joe Singleton Collection*)

Such was the success of the British nightfighters – Mosquitoes alone downed nine raiders attacking mainly London and Bristol during 23-28 March – that Oberst Peltz was forced to persist in using obsolescent Do 217s and other elderly aircraft on night raids on Britain and during April. This resulted in ever greater losses in April. For example, on the night of the 18th/19th,

On 24/25 March 1944, Flg Offs Edward R Hedgecoe and N L Bamford of No 85 Sqn were forced to fly through the fireball created by the sudden explosion of a II./KG 54 Ju 88 that they had been attacking just seconds before. Upon returning to their West Malling base, the true extent of the damage to their NF XII (VY-O) was shockingly revealed (*via Philip Birtles*)

No 456 Sqn's OC, Wg Cdr Keith Mac-Dermott Hampshire DSO, RAAF and his radar operator, Flg Off T Condon, pose beside the remains of a Ju 88A-4 of 6./KG 6 that they had shot down near Walberton, in Sussex, on the night of 24/25 March 1944 in NF XVII HK286/A. Hampshire would go on to score a further six kills (*ARP*)

The shattered remains of Me 410A-1 9K+KH of I./KG 51, which was shot down by Wg Cdr E D Crew DFC* and Wt Off W R Croysdill in a No 96 Sqn Mosquito on 18/19 April 1944. It crashed in the grounds of St Nicholas Church, in Brighton, the pilot, Hauptmann R Pahl, being found dead in the wreckage, whilst the body of his Bordfunker, Feldwebel W Schuberth, was washed up at Friston the following day (*H Tappin via Dr Theo Boiten*)

which saw the last *Steinbock* raid made on London, eight aircraft were destroyed by Mosquitoes. Altogether, Nos 25, 85, 96, 264, 410, 456 and 488 Sqns accounted for 15 bombers during April. In the face of such losses, the short-lived 'Baby Blitz' came to an end the following month.

On 14/15 May over 100 German bombers attacked Bristol, resulting in eight Mosquito nightfighter kills. Three more raiders were downed by Mosquitoes 24 hours later, and on the night of 22/23 May four bombers were destroyed by NF XVIIs during raids on Portsmouth.

With the sting now going out of the *Steinbock* offensive, the spring of 1944 saw the 'powers-that-be' transfer six Mosquito squadrons from Fighter Command to other commands for offensive operations. Four squadrons went to 2nd TAF (Tactical Air Force), No 604 Sqn joining the former on 26 April 1944, followed by No 29 Sqn on 1 May and Nos 410 and 488 Sqns 11 days later. Finally, in May Nos 85 and 157 Sqns were transferred to No 100 Group Bomber Support.

To help replace the gaps left by the departing Mosquito units within Fighter Command, Beaufighter squadrons had begun converting to the de Havilland fighter. One of these was No 406 'Lynx' Sqn, RCAF, which had received its first NF XIIs in April at its Winkleigh, Devon, base. Once transitioned, the unit helped provide the fighter defence for the invasion forces building up along the south coast of England. Its first Mosquito victory occurred on the night of 29/30 April when Wg Cdr D J Williams DFC and Flg Off Kirkpatrick downed two Do 217s off Plymouth. On 14/15 May the unit destroyed one unidentified enemy aircraft, claimed a further three as probables and a fourth damaged. No 406 Sqn re-equipped with the NF XXX in July and returned to night intruder duties

No 25 Sqn pilots and navigators gather around one of the unit's last NF IIs in late 1943 at Predannack. Squadron OC, Wg Cdr Cathcart Michael Wight-Boycott DSO, can be seen with his arms folded (and lacking any headwear) immediately beneath the nose of the Mosquito. He destroyed four enemy aircraft flying Beaufighters before taking command of No 25 Sqn in September 1943. His first Mosquito victory took place on 28/29 May 1944 when he and Plt Off E A Sanders destroyed an Me 410. Wight-Boycott finished the war with a total of seven kills, two damaged and two V1s shot down (*the late Joe Singleton Collection*)

two months later – a development of the NF XIX, the NF XXX was powered by two-stage 1680 hp Merlin 72s, 1710 hp Merlin 76s or 1690 hp Merlin 113s, and fitted with an AI Mk X radar.

The Luftwaffe's final *Steinbock* raid was mounted on 28/29 May, and it resulted in a victory for Wg Cdr C M Wight-Boycott DSO and Flt Lt D W Reid of No 25 Sqn. Having taken off from Coltishall in NF XVII HK257, they were directed by Neatishead GCI station towards a 'bogey' over the North Sea. The contact turned out to be Me 410 9K+KP of KG 51, crewed by Feldwebel Dietrich and Unteroffizier Schaknies, which was returning from a successful intruder mission over the Cambridge area that had seen the crew down a Stirling bomber. Fifty miles off the coast of Cromer, Wight-Boycott caught the Me 410 just above the sea and fired a half-second burst into it from a distance of 700 ft. The intruder fell burning into the water, its funeral pyre being visible for up to 20 miles. On 23/24 June Wight-Boycott added a Ju 188 destroyed to his score.

Although May 1944 marked the end of the ill-fated *Steinbock* raids, the enemy would remain active over the British Isles for months to come, albeit in a much reduced role. Hitler had originally intended for the V1 flying bombs based at remote sites in north-eastern France to form part of the *Steinbock* offensive, but problems delayed their introduction until 13 June 1944, when ten V1s were catapult-launched against London. The V1 was a small, pilotless, aircraft capable of 400 mph at 2500 ft. It was fitted with a 1870-lb high-explosive warhead, which detonated on impact shortly after the pulse-jet had exhausted its fuel over southern England.

Amazingly, frontline fighter squadrons along the south coast of England were not informed of the existence of the V1 (or the 'buzz bomb' or 'Doodlebug' as it became

One of 150 NF IIs delivered to the RAF between April and October 1942 by de Havilland Hatfield, DD744 is seen here with four guns fitted (like the more typically camouflaged all-black NF II parked behind it) in a high-visibility silver finish during its time with either No 1 or 301 Fighter Training Unit (FTU). Later converted from an NF II to a PR II, the fighter was flown to North Africa by the Overseas Aircraft Delivery Unit (OADU) and used by No 60 Sqn, SAAF on the unit's first sortie from Castel Benito, near Tripoli, on 15 February 1943 (*DH via Philip Birtles*)

Typical Mosquito nightfighter cockpit
(*Brian Whitlock Blundell Collection*)

known) until they appeared in the summer skies! However, defensive measures, including 'anti-Diver' patrols, were quickly put into action , and the first V1 to be destroyed by a Mosquito fell to No 54 OTU instructor Flg Off Rayne Schultz during a freelance sortie from Manston on 14/15 June. He flew straight into the debris of the exploding 'buzz-bomb', returning to Manston with little skinning left on his aircraft.

On 25 June Nos 85 and 157 Sqns were transferred south from 100 Group, in Norfolk, to help combat the V1 menace, both units subsequently flying 'anti-Diver' patrols until 20 August, when they resumed bomber support duties. Mosquitoes had their performance boosted for 'anti-Diver' operations through the employment of nitrous oxide injection, which briefly increased the power output of the engines long enough to allow the aircraft to achieve the high speeds needed to catch the V1.

Mosquitoes (and other Allied single-engined fighters) proved very successful against the 'buzz bombs', with the NF XIIIs of No 96 Sqn, based at Ford, downing no fewer than 174 V1s, while No 418 'City of Edmonton' Sqn, RCAF, at Holmesley, Hurn and Middle Wallop, destroyed 83 – all but seven shot down over the sea. Canadian Russ Bannock, who with Bob Bruce had destroyed 18 and one shared V1s by 28 August, recalls;

'Our first V1 destroyed was on 20 June. We vividly recall the occasion when we came up behind the first V1 that we intercepted from behind. Its pulse-jet engine streaming a long flame reminded us of looking straight into a blast furnace. After picking up some small debris from the first V1, we learned to attack from an angle of about 30°. Each one that we destroyed exploded with a vivid white flash which would temporarily blind us until we pulled away from the explosion. There was always a secondary explosion when the V1 hit the sea, which led us to conclude that only the fuel tanks exploded when hit with cannon and machine gun fire, leaving the warhead to explode when it hit the sea. On one occasion we had an amusing experience when we only fired our four .303-in machine guns (we were out of cannon ammo), and we only seemed to damage the autopilot. The V1 did a 180° turn, then the autopilot righted itself and we watched it continue southward and crash on the French coast.

NF XXX RK953 is seen fitted with AI Mk X centimetric radar in a blunt thimble nose radome. This nightfighter development of the NF XIX first appeared in March 1944 and attained service entry with No 219 Sqn three months later. RK953 was one of 26 NF XXXs delivered between April and June 1945 from the Leavesden works, the Mosquito subsequently seeing frontline service with No 151 Sqn until the unit disbanded on 10 October 1946. After a long period in storage, the veteran nightfighter was passed to the RAF's Signals School on 21 August 1950 (*DH*)

'As the V1s often came in salvos of 10 to 20, there was usually a general free for all, with two or three aircraft diving on the same V1. There were four Mosquito squadrons on patrol so there were at least eight aircraft around at any one time. Fearing collision, we agreed that we would turn on our nav lights when we were in a dive. No 418 Sqn continued on V1 patrols until the launching sites were overrun by the advancing 21st Army in August.'

No 96 Sqn's top scorer (and also the RAF's, for that matter) was Sqn Ldr R N Chudleigh DFC, who destroyed an amazing 152 V1s, including six in one night. Other high-scoring squadron pilots included Flt Lt J W Gough with 51 and Flt Lt (later AVM) Frank 'Togs' Mellersh DFC, who destroyed between 39 and 42 V1s (in addition to having eight confirmed 'manned' aircraft kills, seven of them on Beaufighters). No 264 (within the 2nd TAF) Sqn, and Fighter Command's Nos 219, 418, 456 and 605 Sqns, all achieved V1 kills at night.

By the end of June 1944, No 605 Sqn had downed 36 V1s, and it added a further 29 during July. Along with No 418 Sqn, the unit transferred to the 2nd TAF on 21 November. Altogether, Mosquito units accounted for an impressive 471 V1s.

In June No 125 'Newfoundland' Sqn began flying patrols over the French invasion coast. Four months earlier the unit had begun replacing its Beaufighters with the latest version of the Mosquito nightfighter, the NF XVII. It was joined over France from 9 July onwards by No 68 Sqn, who introduced the NF XIX to frontline service 17 days later. At the end of August the Mosquito ranks over the Normandy front were further bolstered with the arrival of No 219 Sqn, which transferred into No 85 (Base) Group, 2nd TAF.

The Allied advance gradually overran the V1 launching sites in the Pas de Calais area of northern France, but this did not entirely eradicate the 'buzz bomb' menace for the Luftwaffe mounted a new terror blitz by air, launching Fieseler Fi 103 flying bombs from beneath the wings of specially-modified Heinkel He 111H-22 bombers.

By August 410 V1s had been air-launched against London, Southampton and Gloucester from Heinkels of III./KG 3, based at Venlo and Gilze Rijen, in Holland. The Heinkels would usually take-off at night, fly low over the North Sea to evade radar and climb to about 1475 ft, before firing their 'stand off' weapons from up to 50 miles off the coast. In Sep-

NF XXX MV529 is prepared for test flying at Leavesden in September 1944. Following its delivery to the RAF, the Mosquito saw service with No 25 Sqn at Castle Camps until it was destroyed in a mid-air collision with fellow squadron aircraft MT494 on 23/24 January 1945. MV259 was crewed by Sqn Ldr J Arnsley DFC and Flt Lt D M Reid DFC at the time of the collision, which occurred over Camps Hall, Cambridgeshire, during an AI practice interception – the second crew involved were Flt Lts D L Ward DFC and E D Eyles (*BAe via Philip Birtles*)

NF XXX NT585 of No 125 Sqn was photographed on 10 December 1945 during a flight from Church Fenton. Mosquito fighters remained in frontline service with Fighter Command until replaced by Meteor NF 11 nightfighters in the early 1950s. Having been initially delivered to Polish-manned No 307 'City of Lvov' Sqn in early 1945, NT585 was passed to No 151 Sqn after its brief spell with No 125. Like many surplus NF XXXs, the fighter ended up with the Signals School in July 1948 (via Philip Birtles)

tember the Allied advance forced III./KG 3 to abandon bases in Holland and move to airfields in Germany. By this stage in the war only the AI-equipped Mosquito nightfighter and Tempest V had proven able to counter the new threat. The first He 111H-22s to be shot down by Mosquitoes fell on the night of 25/26 September when Wt Off Fitchett and Flt Sgt Hardy of No 409 Sqn (in NF XIII MM589) and Flg Off Beadle of No 25 Sqn each destroyed a Heinkel over the North Sea.

Over the next three months a further 17 He 111H-22s were destroyed by NF XVIIs, XXXs and XIXs of Nos 25, 125, 68 and 456 Sqns, as well as the FIU. The last victim to fall to the Mosquitoes was downed on 6 January 1945 when No 68 Sqn's Wt Off A Brooking and Plt Off Finn used HK296 to destroy a He 111H-22 over the North Sea – their NF XVII must have been hit during the encounter, or suffered engine problems as a result of the engagement, however, for the crew failed to return.

During the final months of the war, Nos 25, 68, 96, 125, 151, 307, 406 and 456 Sqns all flew Bomber Support, 'Lure' and intruder operations to pre-selected airfields on the other side of 'bomb line' in Germany. During Bomber Support operations, the objective was to protect the bombers from attack by enemy fighters from airfields adjacent to the target area. Mosquito crews timed their arrival some ten minutes prior to the coloured TIs (Target Indicators) being dropped by the Pathfinders, and the subsequent arrival of the main bomber force. They would then orbit their allocated airfields. They would continue to do this while the actual bombing took place, navigators keeping a watchful eye on the AI Mk X radar tube for any activity taking place below them.

Operation 'Lure' was designed to intercept enemy fighters attempting to follow RAF heavy bombers returning from their targets. Mosquito pilots would join the rear of the stream and then throttle back and lower a few degrees of flap to simulate the bomber's speed. The navigator, using the rear facing Monica system, would watch for any unidentified aircraft approaching. In the event of a 'bogey' being detected, it was 'open throttles, raise flaps, smart 180° turn, make contact with Mk X radar and intercept', or perhaps I should say 'investigate' – sometimes, the contact turned out to be a crippled Lancaster or Halifax.

Whilst on Bomber Support operations, crews would also carry out the strafing of pre-selected airfields, and despite the dangerous nature of these operations, Mosquito nightfighters were very much the aggressors, giving their Luftwaffe counterparts far greater cause for concern (see *Osprey Aircraft of the Aces 20 - German Nightfighter Aces* for further details).

OFFENSIVE NIGHTFIGHTING

Offensive nightfighting had been pioneered in June 1940 by Blenheim squadrons in much the same way that Sopwith Camel-equipped No 151 Sqn had done in World War 1. In November 1939 No 600 'City of London' Sqn had become one of the first units to use AI (Airborne Interception) radar (No 604 'County of Middlesex' Sqn followed suit in July 1940). When the Luftwaffe began operating at night from France in 1940, the opportunity of attacking aircraft on French airfields arose, but the only suitable aircraft then available were Hurricanes, Blenheims and, later, Havocs and Bostons.

By 1942 Bomber Command had begun to suffer steadily increasing losses to Luftwaffe nightfighters, and it was felt that RAF intruder aircraft roving over enemy airfields in France and the Low Countries could help reduce some of these attacks on the bomber streams. The first major support of bombers by nightfighter units came on the night of 30/31 May 1942 during the 1000 bomber raid on Cologne, when Blenheims, Hav-

Mosquitoes were ideal for Intruder operations, but in 1942 squadrons re-equipping from other types had to use converted NF IIs bereft of the still secret Mk IV radar, but with increased fuel capacity (*via Mick Jennings*)

ocs and Boston IIIs of Nos 23 and 418 'City of Edmonton' Sqns 'intruded' over Holland – in February 1943 the latter unit converted to the Mosquito. No radar-equipped aircraft were used on this occasion, as the use of AI equipment over enemy territory was still banned.

The Mosquito was ideally suited to the Intruder mission, and by 1943 the FB VI (see *Osprey Combat Aircraft 4 - Mosquito Bomber/Fighter-Bomber Units 1942-45* for FB VI bomber operations) would allow sorties to be flown as far afield as Austria and Czechoslovakia. However, in 1942 squadrons re-equipping from other types had to soldier on with modified NF IIs fitted with extra fuel tanks and bereft of their AI Mk IV radar. As there were few NF IIs that could be spared at this stage of the war, any Mosquitoes that were available were welcomed, whatever their pedigree.

Starting in March 1943, 'C' Flight of No 85 Sqn at Hunsdon was presented with five NF XV high-altitude fighters, which had been pressed into service in response to the threat posed by the Ju 86 high-altitude bomber. The prototype (MP469) was the first Mosquito built to feature a pressurised cabin, and it completed its maiden flight on 8 August 1942.

Later fitted with AI Mk VIII radar (as were the remaining four NF XVs), the aircraft was essentially a modified B IVs married to two two-stage 1680 hp Merlin 72/73 or 1710 hp 76/77 engines, driving three or four-bladed airscrews. Capable of reaching heights of 43,000 ft+, the NF XV was armed with four .303-in machine guns in an under-belly pack. In August the NF XVs were re-allocated to Farnborough for use in pressure cabin research, and that same month No 85 Sqn finally began Intruder patrols with the NF II. They would have to wait until 19 October, however, before getting their first scent of a kill, when Flt Lt E N Bunting and Flg Off C P Reed claimed a Ju 88 damaged and Sgt Clunes and Plt Off Jones probably destroyed a Do 217.

The same state of affairs concerning conversion to the NF II persisted at Colerne, where in May 1942 No 264 'Madras Presidency' Sqn began their conversion from Defiant IIs – its first Mosquito, a T III, arrived on the 3rd, and on 13 June the unit flew its first operational sorties using NF IIs. Late in 1942, what few NF IIs were available carried out night Rangers to airfields in France. 'Rangers' were low-level operations flown

Right
In July 1942 No 23 Sqn began converting from Boston Is and Havoc IIIs to Mosquito NF IIs at Ford, the unit eventually receiving 25 suitably-modified de Havilland fighters. This particular aircraft is DZ238, which was nicknamed 'Babs' during its time with the unit. Issued to No 23 Sqn as new in October 1942, DZ238 was retained until the unit transferred to Malta in late December, whereupon it was passed firstly to No 60 OTU, followed by No 13 OTU. It was finally struck off charge in November 1945 (*via Kelvin Sloper*)

MP469 was the prototype NF XV high-altitude fighter, boasting the the first pressurised cabin fitted to a Mosquito. It completed its maiden flight on 8 August 1942, and was later fitted with an AI Mk VIII radar. A further four NF XVs (all modified B IVs with two-stage 1680 hp Merlin 72/73 or 1710 hp 76/77 engines) were built, all of which saw very brief operational service with 'C' Flight of No 85 Sqn in March 1943. This particular aircraft was reduced in status to a ground instructional airframe at the end of September 1944. Note the NF XV's distinctive four-bladed propellers and extended wing span (*GMS*)

on moonlight nights mainly against railway rolling stock and road transport, although enemy aircraft were also shot down if encountered.

Nightly, No 264 Sqn would also patrol the West Country, and by day they operated over the Bay of Biscay and the Western Approaches on 'Instep' sorties. On 27/28 June a Do 217 was claimed as 'damaged', followed 24 hours later by the unit's first combat success with the NF II when Flg Off A J Hodgkinson downed KG 2's Unteroffizier Rudolf Blankenburg as he made for Creil in a Do 217E-2 after raiding Weston-Super-Mare. In 1943 No 264 Sqn switched totally to night intruding from the Cornish coastal airfield at Preddanack, concentrating on patrolling over Laon and Juvencourt.

In July 1942 Ford-based No 23 Sqn (which had received a T III for conversion purposes on 7 June) began replacing its Boston IIIs with Mosquito NF IIs. However, because these aircraft were desperately needed to equip home defence squadrons opposing the *Baedeker* raids, it took some considerable period of time for the No 23 Sqn to receive its quota of 25 modified NF IIs. Indeed, for a time the unit boasted just one available Mosquito for intruding duties – DD670/'S-Sugar'.

Appropriately, the unit's first NF II Intruder sortie was flown in this aircraft on 5/6 July by its OC, the inimitable Wg Cdr Bertie Rex O'Bryen Hoare DSO DFC*, accompanied by Plt Off Cornes. 'Sammy' Hoare, who sported a large handlebar moustache reputedly 'six inches, wingtip to wingtip', was one of the leading intruder pilots of his generation, having flown first Blenheims, then Havocs, on intruder sorties over the Low Countries. He succinctly described Intruder operations thus;

'I should like to tell you not to measure the value of this night-

fighter work over German aerodromes by the number of enemy aircraft destroyed. This is considerable, but our mere presence over the bases has caused the loss of German bombers without a shot being fired at them.'

'Sammy' Hoare's first NF II sortie proved somewhat uneventful, as no sightings were made. However, on the following night (6/7 July) he and Plt Off Cornes despatched a Do 217 16 miles east of Chartres with three short bursts of cannon fire. On 8/9 July Sqn Ldr K H Salisbury-Hughes used 'S-Sugar' to destroy a Do 217 over Etampes and a He 111 at Evreux, and finally on 30/31 July 'Sammy' Hoare again enjoyed success with the aircraft when he downed an unidentified enemy aircraft (UEA) at Orleans. Intruding was dangerous work, and as 'Sammy' Hoare wrote;

'Nightfighter pilots chosen for intruder work were generally of a different type to the ordinary fighter pilot. They must like nightfighting to begin with, which is not everybody's meat. They must also have the technique for blind flying, and when it comes to fighting, must use their own initiative and judgement, since they are cut off from all communications with their base and are left as freelances entirely to their own resources.'

On 8/9 September three NF IIs were lost on Intruder sorties over the Continent. Then, two nights later 'Sammy' Hoare and J F Potter, flying 'B-Bertie', destroyed another UEA south of Enschede. On occasion No 157 Sqn at Castle Camps also flew NF II sorties over the continent, and on 30 September Wg Cdr R F H Clerke used DD607 to destroy a Ju 88A-4 30 miles off the Dutch coast.

In December 1942 No 23 Sqn was posted to Malta for Intruder operations against the Axis. 'Sammy' Hoare, having raised his wartime tally to six confirmed, had left the unit prior to its departure overseas to set up a specialised Intruder training 'school' at No 51 OTU at Cranfield, in Bedfordshire.

As the first of five Mosquito fighter units to see action in the Mediterranean and Italy, No 23 Sqn was sent to Luqa, on Malta, in late December 1942. Enjoying much success in Intruder operations against the Axis, one of the unit's initial complement of aircraft was DZ230/YP-A, seen here overflying Valetta Harbour with No 23 Sqn OC, Wg Cdr Peter G Wykeham-Barnes DSO DFC, at the controls in January 1943. Having already scored 12 kills on Hurricanes and Gladiators in North Africa in 1940-41, Wykeham-Barnes added a further two kills and a damaged to his tally with the Mosquito in 1943. DZ230 was amongst a clutch of brand new NF IIs supplied to the unit in the autumn of 1942, and was subsequently written off when it overshot on landing at Luqa on 22 June 1943 (*ARP*)

The first victory to fall to No 23 Sqn in the Mediterranean was a Ju 88 claimed by Sqn Ldr Philip Russell (left) and Plt Off E G Pullen on 8 January during an Intruder to Tunis airfield. The unit operated from Luqa with NF IIs from late December 1942 through to May 1943 (with detachments at Pomigliano and Alghero), when it received FB VIs. It continued to fly Intruder sorties against the Axis in Italy, North Africa and Sicily until posted back to the UK in June 1944 (*via Tom Cushing*)

No 23 Sqn would not return to the UK until the end of June 1944, when they joined No 100 Group.

In February 1943 No 605 'County of Warwick' Sqn at Bradwell Bay began replacing its Bostons and Havocs with NF IIs. One of the unit's first successful missions took place on 4/5 May when six Mosquito night intruders patrolled over Dutch airfields awaiting the arrival of Luftwaffe bombers returning from a raid on Norwich. Flg Off Brian Williams and Plt Off Dougie Moore duly shot down Do 217E-4 (Wk-Nr 4353) U5+CK of III./KG 2, piloted by Lt Ernst Andres, which was returning to its base at Eindhoven. Andres crash-landed at Landsmere, near Amsterdam, and among the dead aboard the bomber was Major Walter Bradel, *Kommodore* of KG 2 – Andres recovered from injuries sustained in the crash, only to be killed flying with V./NJG 4 on 11 February 1945. A second Do 217 flown by Unteroffizier Hügler of II./KG 52, was also downed near Eindhoven almost certainly by Williams and Moore.

On 16 February 1943 No 151 Sqn (which had re-equipped with the NF II at Wittering in April 1942) also began night intruder operations over France flying Mosquitoes fitted with the tail warning device Monica. The unit upgraded to NF XIIs in May, and continued to fly night Ranger operations over the continent with this mark until April 1944.

February 1943 also saw No 410 Sqn, RCAF move south from Acklington to Castle Camps with its NF IIs for moonlight night Ranger operations. As the third Canadian nightfighter unit to be formed in June 1941, the 'Cougar' squadron had commenced the transition from Beaufighter IIFs to Mosquitoes in October 1942.

The first intruder operation flown by the unit took place on 26 February, and the Canadians also flew Day Rangers as well. The dangers appertaining to the latter operations were borne out on 6 April when Flt Lt C D McCloskey (one of the squadron's original members) and Plt Off J G Sullivan failed to return from a sortie. German radio later announced that they had been shot down and were PoWs – four days later Flg Offs J E Leach and R M Bull were killed in action over Friesland.

Ranger operations began again when the moon period arrived in mid-April, and on the night of the 15th, No 410 Sqn's OC, Wg Cdr Frank W Hillock, headed for the Ruhr. The weather was poor and, as the Mosquito

Seen at Malta in casual attire, Wg Cdr A M 'Sticky' Murphy DSO, DFC, C de G was No 23 Sqn's OC from December 1943 through to December 1944. He was killed on an Intruder to Gütersloh on 2 December 1944, his position then being filled by Wg Cdr Philip Russell (*via Tom Cushing*)

No 151 Sqn's NF II DD609 is seen in characteristic all-black finish fitted with AI radar. On 16 February 1943 the unit (which had re-equipped with the NF II at Wittering in April 1942) began night intruder operations over France flying Mosquitoes fitted with the tail warning device known as Monica. DD609 survived its tour with No 151 Sqn and was posted to No 54 OTU in mid-1943. It was finally stuck off charge in June 1945 (*via GMS*)

skipped along at 300 ft over Holland, Hillock suddenly saw the eight radio masts of Apeldoorn station rushing towards him. There was no time to climb, and no room to fly between them, so he threw the Mosquito onto its side and ripped through the antennae, tearing away several wires. Upon returning to Coleby Grange, it was found that one wing tip had been sliced off, and the other wing had been cut through to the main spar before the wire had broken – 300 ft of well-made copper cable was also trailing behind the Mosquito! Despite this shaking experience, Hillock had coolly flown to his target before coming home. The wing commander completed his tour on 20 May and was succeeded by Wg Cdr G H Elms.

Over the next four nights No 410 Sqn crews located a convoy off the Dutch coast which proved suitable for a naval attack, and strafed barges in Holland, a factory in Rees and railyards at Cleve. On 20 April Flt Sgt W J Reddie and Sgt Evans went missing, however. There then followed a week of poor weather which ruled out further Rangers, but during the moon period in May, the unit flew operations over both France and Belgium. Between 14-29 May No 410 Sqn flew 10 midnight Intruder and 14 Night Ranger sorties, as well patrolling enemy airfields in support of Bomber Command operations, although the latter proved uneventful.

Seven of the Ranger crews found targets to attack during this period, which comprised mainly locomotives and their wagons. Indeed, 14 locomotives and 11 freight cars were claimed as destroyed, as well as several barges. One crew ('Butch' Bouchard and his navigator Fyfe) enjoyed astounding success in the Dummer Lake area on 15 May when they claimed five locomotives and no less than 112 freight cars destroyed!

June was far quieter and less eventful as far as scrambles and Rangers were concerned. However, Coastal Command anti-submarine operations in the Bay of Biscay were being hampered by enemy counter-air activity, so No 410 Sqn was requested to supply fighter support. Four crews were detached to Predannack for 'Instep' patrols (another squadron intruder detachment was also temporarily established at Hunsdon), where they joined Polish crews from No 307 Sqn, who had also begun flying Night Rangers, and No 456 Sqn, RAAF. The 'Cougar' crews

NF II DZ716/UP-L of No 605 Sqn is seen in flight in the spring of 1943. In February of that year the Bradwell Bay-based unit had begun replacing its Bostons and Havocs with NF IIs. The squadron flew its first successful mission on the night of 4/5 May when six Mosquito night intruders patrolled over Dutch airfields awaiting the arrival of Luftwaffe bombers returning from a raid on Norwich. Flg Off Brian Williams and Plt Off Dougie Moore duly shot down Do 217E-4 (Wk-Nr 4353) U5+CK of III./KG 2, piloted by Leutnant Ernst Andres, which was returning to its Eindhoven base. Two more Do 217M-1s were destroyed by NF IIs of No 605 Sqn on 13/14 and 25/26 July 1943. By that stage, however, DD716 had itself been destroyed in a crash-landing at Castle Camps on 7 July (via Ron Mackay)

remained at Preddanack for a month, flying 20 patrols in that time which lasted between four and five hours' duration. On the afternoon of the 13th, Plt Off R B Harris and Sgt E H Skeel, along with by three other Mosquitoes, intercepted a formation of four Ju 88s on a patrol south-west of Brest. The arrival of Fw 190s on the scene soon swung the action in favour of the Luftwaffe, however, and three aircraft, including the No 410 Sqn Mosquito were shot down.

The next morning, Plt Offs J Watt and E H Collis, along with three Polish crews, sighted five U-boats in the Bay of Biscay, which drew into a tight defensive circle once they had spotted the Mosquitoes. Two of the aircraft attacked the U-boats, which peppered the sky with flak, and strikes were seen on the conning towers of both submarines. In return, one Mosquito was damaged by flak, although all the aircraft returned to Predannack.

On 19 June, during yet another combined patrol involving Canadian and Polish aircraft, Flg Offs E A Murray and P R Littlewood of No 410 Sqn encountered a Blohm und Voss Bv 138 flying boat at low level over the Bay of Biscay. The Mosquitoes made two line astern attacks on the Bv 138, which attempted to climb into cloud On the first attack one engine was hit and began to smoke, preventing the aircraft from gaining height, and forcing its pilot to nose down towards the water. On the second attack the starboard engine was hit and caught fire, the aircraft then crashing into the sea. Three crew emerged and scrambled into a dinghy.

The last action occurred on 21 June when Plt Off C F Green and Sgt E G White participated in a patrol which attacked two small armed merchant vessels, or trawlers, damaging both.

The first half of 1943 had seen a number of units convert onto the now more readily-abundant nightfighter Mosquito. No 456 Sqn (which had been involved in the June 'Instep' operations) had flown Beaufighters since September 1941, and it started to receive its first NF IIs in December 1942. By February-March 1943 the unit had begun to include Ranger operations in addition to its day fighting role, firstly from Middle Wallop and then from Colerne, and by late May they were successfully employed on Intruder sorties over France, attacking railway rolling stock and intruding over airfields. That same month both Ford-based No 256 Sqn and Bradwell Bay-based No 29 Sqn also converted from Beaufighter VIFs to Mosquito NF XIIs.

No 264 Sqn crews discuss last minute details of the night's sortie before clambering aboard their NF IIs at Predannack in the autumn of 1943. The unit had flown its first operational sorties with the Mosquito on 13 June 1943, being joined in this role in August by No 85 Sqn and their NF IIs. Few Mosquito nightfighters could be spared for this role at this stage in the war, and the veritable handful of NF IIs that were made available carried out low level night Rangers to airfields across western France

No 410 Sqn's Flt Lt Rayne 'Joe' Dennis Schultz DFC*, from Bashow, Alberta, and Flg Off Vernon A Williams DFC pose for the camera at Coleby Grange. They scored their first victory (in FB VI HP849) on 15/16 August 1943, and on the night of 10/11 December shot down three Do 217s into the North Sea between Clacton and Dunkirk in NF II DZ292. Schultz later teamed up with Flg Off J S Christie to score four more victories flying NF XIIIs and XXXs before the end of the war (*Stephen M Fochuk*)

May 1943 had also seen No 60 OTU at High Ercall, in Shropshire, expanded and made responsible for all Intruder training. On 7/8 May No 418 Sqn (then still predominantly equipped with Bostons and Havocs) flew its first Mosquito sortie from Ford, Plt Off Tony Croft claiming a Ju 88 destroyed in the Melun-Britigny area during the mission. Later that month the unit accepted its first FB VIs, and on 27/28 June Sqn Ldr C C Moran proved the versatility of the fighter-bomber by claiming a Ju 88 and an He 111 destroyed at Avord, plus a train and a radio mast blown up by his bombs during the same sortie. By the end of the summer Moran had earned himself a deserved reputation as a 'train-buster', his technique usually consisting of a strafing run to stop the locomotive, before finishing it off with his bombs.

Flt Lt Tim Woodman, who flew Beaufighters and Mosquitoes on intruder operations during this period, also 'train-busted';

'Individually in the moonlight we crossed the Channel into France. The French Resistance informed us that the midnight train out of Paris to Rouen was normally packed with troops returning from leave. Shooting up the engines resulted in the first passenger coaches also being hit. The Resistance then informed us that, because of this, the rear coaches were reserved for officers, so we shot up the engine (steam would sprout out like hosepipes and the engines would be put out of action, blocking the line for a time), then came round again and shot up the rear coaches.'

Aside from the several units undertaking 'Instep' patrols from Predannack, the base was also used by a detachment of No 25 Sqn NF IIs attached to No 264 Sqn – the former unit had received NF IIs in October 1942 and started freelance Ranger sweeps over the continent soon after.

June 1943 also saw Mosquitoes from Nos 456 and 605 Sqns commencing successful (albeit on a small-scale) Bomber Support 'Flower' attacks on German nightfighter airfields during raids by main force bombers. 'Flowers' supported bombers by disrupting enemy Flying Control Organisations, long-range Intruder aircraft fitted with limited radar equipment being employed for the task. These aircraft would proceed to the target at high altitude, diving down whenever they could see airfields illuminated. This type of operation, if correctly timed, prevented enemy nightfighters already short of petrol from landing at their bases.

One Mosquito crew rapidly making a name for themselves on offensive nightfighting patrols at this time comprised Flt Lts James Gillies Benson DFC and Lewis Brandon DSO, DFC of No 157 Sqn. On 12/13 June, flying NF XIX MM630, they destroyed a Ju 188 over the Foret de Compeigne, and on the night of 3/4 July, using NF II DD739, they downed a Do 217 over St Trond. On 13/14 July Flg Off Smart of No 605 Sqn, flying an NF II, destroyed a Do 217M-1 near Eindhoven. Nos 456 and 605 Sqns also re-equipped with the FB VIs for Intruding during July, whilst

No 418 Sqn completed the last of its Boston sorties and switched entirely to 'Flower' operations with the FB VI instead.

Earlier that same month No 410 Sqn had also received six FB VIs for use on Intruder and Ranger operations, and in August six more FB VIs and six NF IIs were made available for 'Flowers' operations. The unit lost Plt Off L A Wood and Flg Off D J Slaughter during a Night Ranger to France from Ford on 18 July, and poor weather prevented any further operations until the night of 25 July, when two 'Cougar' crews flew 'Flower' sorties to Deelen airfield, in Holland. Once over the target area, Flt Lt Murray and Flg Off Littlewood orbited a dummy airfield for a few moments before spotting an aircraft coming in to land. Thirty seconds later another contact appeared, flicking its navigation lights on and off. The FB VI crew quickly came in behind what turned out to be a Do 217 and fired a three-second burst at the aircraft. Searchlights coned the Mosquito while flak guns opened up, although by this time the Dornier's port engine had caught fire. Fixed in the beams of five searchlights, the bomber veered to the left before exploding in flames on the airfield boundary.

As the FB VI crew continued to circle the airfield, a third aircraft made a hurried landing, and on reaching the end of the runway the navigation lights were turned on. Murray came down in a sharp diving turn and fired a long burst at the aircraft, damaging it. The navigation lights were quickly doused and the ground defences opened up again.

In August it was realised that the Luftwaffe were operating radar-equipped nightfighters against the 'heavies' of Bomber Command. AI-equipped Beaufighters and Mosquito nightfighters were therefore released over enemy territory on 'Mahmoud' operations as bait for enemy nightfighters in their known assembly areas. With centimetre AI radar being used in Mosquitoes, it was necessary to fit Monica tail warning devices, as the later marks of AI did not scan to the rear. Using Mosquitoes as fake bombers did not prove to be overly successful, however, as the enemy soon recognised their speed difference.

Nevertheless, a few victories were recorded over the continent during the month, notably on 15/16 August a double Do 217M-1 haul by Flt Sgt Brearley in a NF XII from No 256 Sqn.

As briefly mentioned in chapter one, on that same night in August, Flg Offs Rayne Dennis Schultz and

Revealing just how closely together the pilot and navigator/radar operator sat in the cockpit of the Mosquito, Battle of Britain veteran Michael Hugh Constable-Maxwell (right) and Sgt John Quinton are seen in their No 264 Sqn NF II. The pair damaged a Do 217 on 21/22 January 1943 and claimed a 'probable' IV./KG 1 He 111 on 30 March. They then moved to No 604 Sqn where, after a spell on Beaufighters, they gained four confirmed Mosquito kills between March and July 1944, raising Constable-Maxwell's final score to six and one shared destroyed. Promoted to wing commander and flight lieutenant respectively, Constable-Maxwell DSO DFC and Quinton DFC remained a crew throughout the latter's time as OC No 84 Sqn in Java in 1946-47. Sadly, Quinton was killed in a Wellington crash on 13 August 1951 (*via Ron MacKay*)

V A Williams of No 410 Sqn set off from Castle Camps in FB VI HP849 on a Ranger, but did not reach their intended target – the airfield at St Dizier. Instead, they attacked three locomotives between Clermont and Poix, and bombed a bridge. On the way home, some 20 minutes off Beachy Head, they spotted another aircraft, and on closing discovered it was a Do 217M-1. The enemy belly gunner opened accurate fire on the FB VI whilst his pilot tried to shake off their pursuer. A long chase followed until the Canadian's second burst hit the cockpit, where fires broke out and debris fell away. Three or four crewmen were then seen to bale out before the Dornier turned for France in a shallow, controlled dive. Schultz fired again and the starboard wing and engine broke away. Enveloped in flames, the bomber hit the sea and burned brightly. After taking some cine films of the scene, and reporting the position of the crew, Schultz and Williams headed for home to report their first victory.

Two nights later, on the 17th/18th, Flt Lt D H Blomely of No 605 Sqn destroyed a Bf 109 east of Schleswig, and on 22/23 August a No 29 Sqn NF XII crew used HK164 to down an Me 410A-1 north of Knocke. Blomely was credited with a second victory on 21 September when he destroyed two Ju 88s west of the Skaggerak.

On the 24th No 410 Sqn started 'Mahmoud' operations, although these remained unsuccessful until the night of 27/28 September when Flt Lt M A Cybulski and Flg Off H H Ladbrook, flying NF II DZ757, patrolled the Zeider Zee and Meppen areas from Coleby Grange. The 90-minute sortie over the Continent was unsuccessful, but on the way home an AI contact was made on a Do 217 which was then located flying east. The enemy pilot went into a steep climb with the Mosquito closing

On 12/13 June 1943 No 157 Sqn's Flt Lts James Gillies Benson DFC (second left) and Lewis Brandon DSO DFC (centre) used NF XIX MM630 to destroy a Ju 188 over the Foret de Compeigne, followed by a Do 217 over St Trond on 3/4 July in NF II DD739. They are seen here with Flt Lt Barry Hull, Brian Blundell and his navigator, Gilbert 'Gib' Davidson, at Predannack in 1943 (*Brian Whitlock Blundell Collection*)

No 157 Sqn began re-equipping with FB VIs at Hunsdon in July 1943, and they used the aircraft predominantly on intruder operations. This particular Mosquito (HP850) was one of 500 built by prewar car manufacturer Standard Motors of Coventry between June 1943 and December 1944, and was amongst the first batch of FB VIs delivered to No 157 Sqn at Hunsdon. It saw only brief service with the unit, however, for it was passed to the 2nd TAF's Australian-manned No 464 Sqn at Sculthorpe in the early autumn. HP850 was subsequently lost on a low-level bombing raid to Metz/Woippy on 9 October 1943 (*Brian Whitlock Blundell Collection*)

rapidly, although a three-second burst from the NF II was enough to see the bomber explode with a terrific flash and descend enveloped in flames. Burning petrol and oil 'roasted' the Mosquito, scorching the fuselage from nose to tail, the port wing inboard of the engine, the bottom of the starboard wing, the port tailplane and rudder. Pieces of the Dornier struck the port oil cooler, resulting in the loss of oil, and making it necessary to shut down the engine. Cybulski was blinded and Ladbrook had to take control for five minutes until the pilot regained his vision. Course was set for base, and the seriously damaged aircraft completed a hazardous 250-mile single-engine return. The crew received immediate DFCs.

By September 1943 No 605 Sqn were flying Intruder sorties over Denmark and Germany. That same month, 'Sammy' Hoare assumed command of the unit, and he returned to operations on 27/28 September, whereupon he promptly despatched a Do 217 at Dedelsdorf for his seventh air-to-air kill – on 10/11 January 1944 Hoare scored No 605 Sqn's 100th victory when he and Flg Off Robert C Muir downed a Ju 188 east of Chievres. 'Sammy' claimed a probable and three aircraft damaged in 1944, plus 'bagged' his ninth, and last, kill in March of that year.

Intruder victories were now becoming hard to get, with none being recorded until Flt Lt Blomely DFC destroyed a Bf 110 west of Aalborg on 9 November, followed by a Bf 110 at Mannheim ten days later, claimed by Wg Cdr Roderick A Chisholm DFC and Flt Lt F C Clarke of the FIU in NF II HJ705. That same month a No 307 Sqn detachment at Sumburgh, in Scotland, carried out 'Rhubarbs' over Norway, destroying two He 177s and a Ju 88. Upon returning south, they continued intruding and later flew Bomber Support operations until March 1945.

By November 'Bomber Support' had become the 'buzz word' in offensive night fighting, and starting on the 23rd, Fighter Command had to give up Beaufighter and Mosquito squadrons upon the formation of No 100 Group (Special Duties, later Bomber Support – see chapter five). Since the formation of 2nd Tactical Air Force in June 1943, greater emphasis also began to be placed on the offensive capabilities of the night-fighter squadrons, because the new command also had the task of invasion support in the run-up to Operation *Overlord*, which was scheduled for mid-1944.

COLOUR PLATES

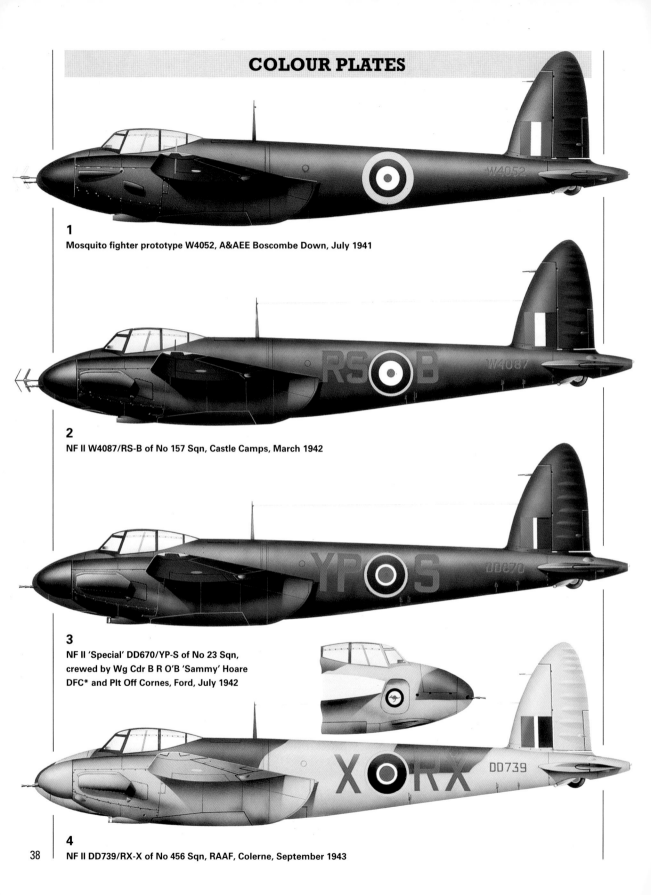

1
Mosquito fighter prototype W4052, A&AEE Boscombe Down, July 1941

2
NF II W4087/RS-B of No 157 Sqn, Castle Camps, March 1942

3
NF II 'Special' DD670/YP-S of No 23 Sqn, crewed by Wg Cdr B R O'B 'Sammy' Hoare DFC* and Plt Off Cornes, Ford, July 1942

4
NF II DD739/RX-X of No 456 Sqn, RAAF, Colerne, September 1943

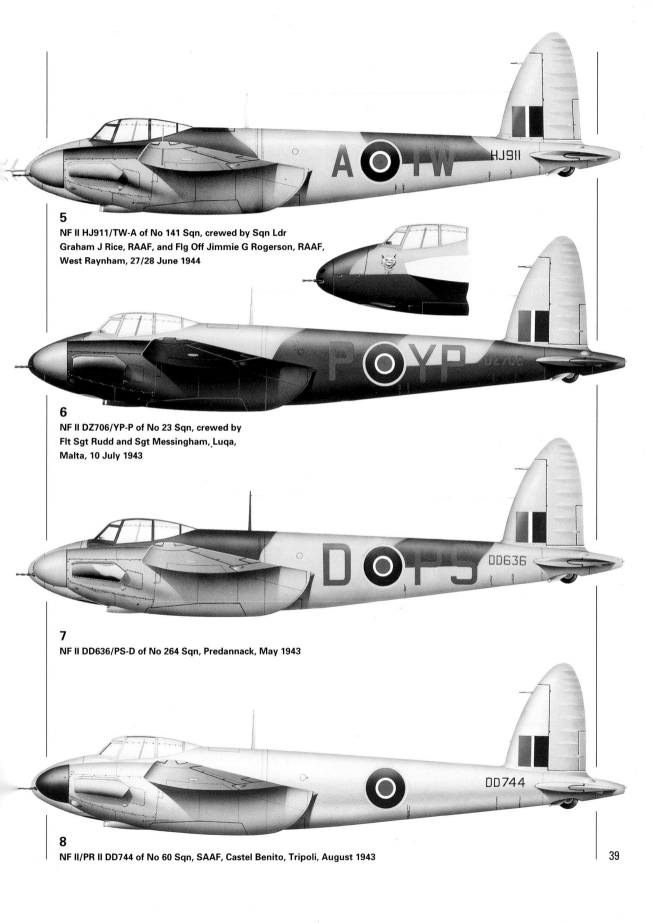

5
NF II HJ911/TW-A of No 141 Sqn, crewed by Sqn Ldr
Graham J Rice, RAAF, and Flg Off Jimmie G Rogerson, RAAF,
West Raynham, 27/28 June 1944

6
NF II DZ706/YP-P of No 23 Sqn, crewed by
Flt Sgt Rudd and Sgt Messingham, Luqa,
Malta, 10 July 1943

7
NF II DD636/PS-D of No 264 Sqn, Predannack, May 1943

8
NF II/PR II DD744 of No 60 Sqn, SAAF, Castel Benito, Tripoli, August 1943

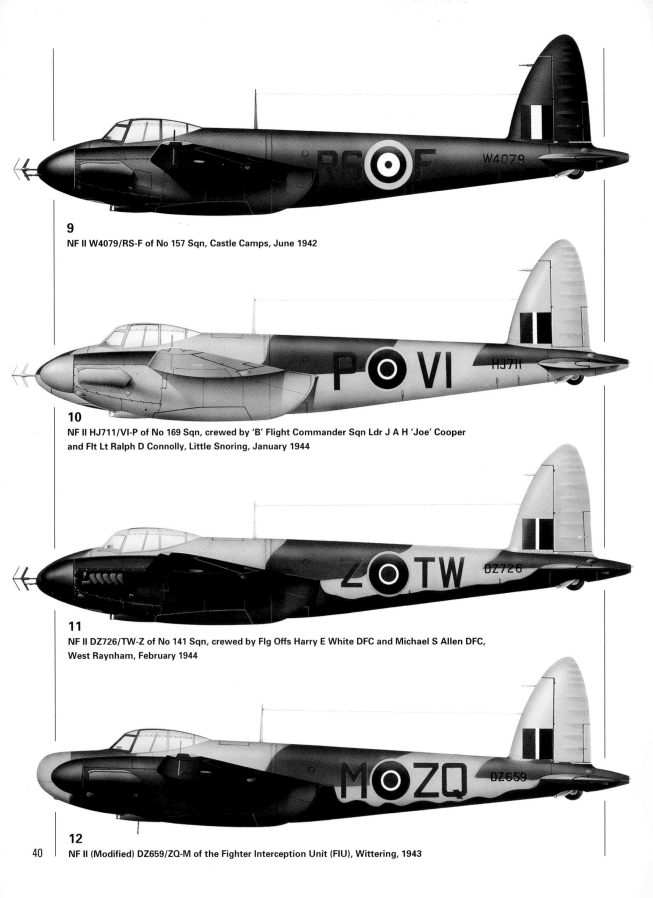

9
NF II W4079/RS-F of No 157 Sqn, Castle Camps, June 1942

10
NF II HJ711/VI-P of No 169 Sqn, crewed by 'B' Flight Commander Sqn Ldr J A H 'Joe' Cooper and Flt Lt Ralph D Connolly, Little Snoring, January 1944

11
NF II DZ726/TW-Z of No 141 Sqn, crewed by Flg Offs Harry E White DFC and Michael S Allen DFC, West Raynham, February 1944

12
NF II (Modified) DZ659/ZQ-M of the Fighter Interception Unit (FIU), Wittering, 1943

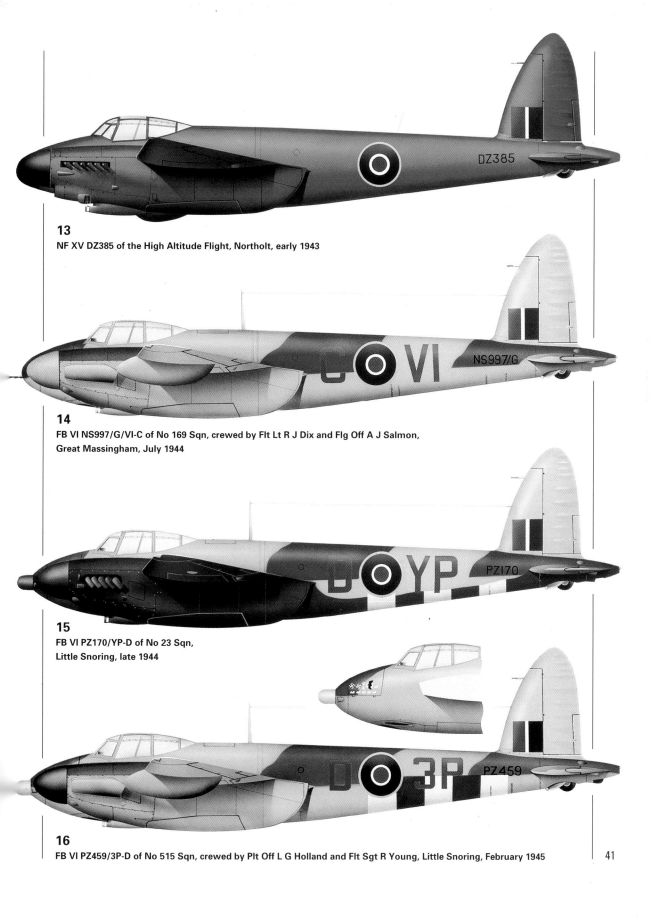

13
NF XV DZ385 of the High Altitude Flight, Northolt, early 1943

14
FB VI NS997/G/VI-C of No 169 Sqn, crewed by Flt Lt R J Dix and Flg Off A J Salmon,
Great Massingham, July 1944

15
FB VI PZ170/YP-D of No 23 Sqn,
Little Snoring, late 1944

16
FB VI PZ459/3P-D of No 515 Sqn, crewed by Plt Off L G Holland and Flt Sgt R Young, Little Snoring, February 1945

17
FB VI NT137/TH-T *Lady Luck* of No 418 'City of Edmonton' Sqn, crewed by Flt Lt Jack H Phillips DFC, RCAF, and Flg Off Bernard M Job, RAFVR, Hartford Bridge, February 1945

18
NF XII HK119/VY-S of No 85 Sqn, crewed by Flt Lt J P M Lintott and Plt Off G G Gilling-Lax, West Malling, May 1943

19
NF XIII MM469/NG-X of No 604 'County of Middlesex' Sqn, Lille/Vendeville, France, early 1945

20
NF XIII MM446/RO-Q of No 29 Sqn, Hunsdon, December 1944

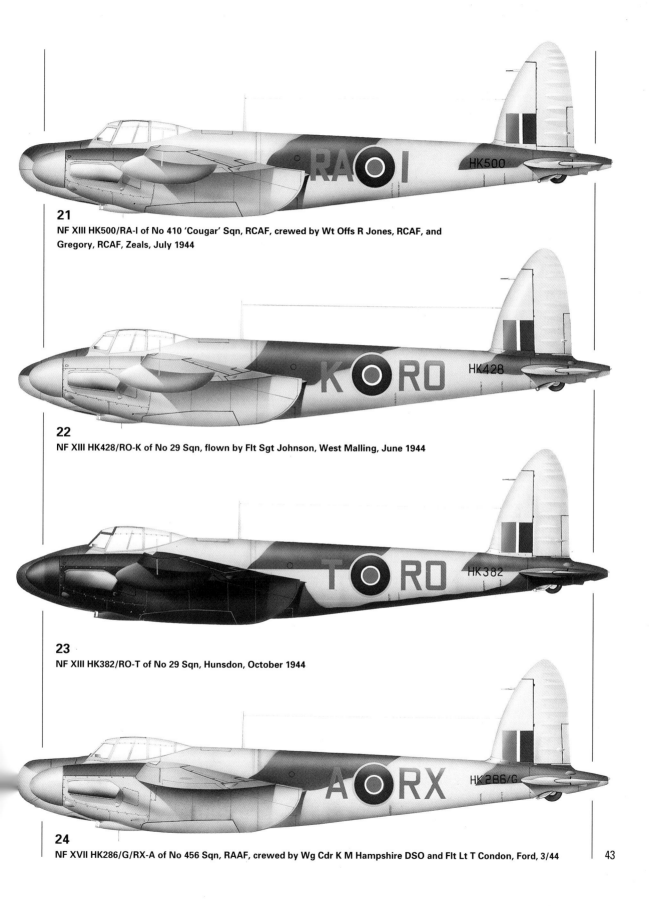

21
NF XIII HK500/RA-I of No 410 'Cougar' Sqn, RCAF, crewed by Wt Offs R Jones, RCAF, and Gregory, RCAF, Zeals, July 1944

22
NF XIII HK428/RO-K of No 29 Sqn, flown by Flt Sgt Johnson, West Malling, June 1944

23
NF XIII HK382/RO-T of No 29 Sqn, Hunsdon, October 1944

24
NF XVII HK286/G/RX-A of No 456 Sqn, RAAF, crewed by Wg Cdr K M Hampshire DSO and Flt Lt T Condon, Ford, 3/44

43

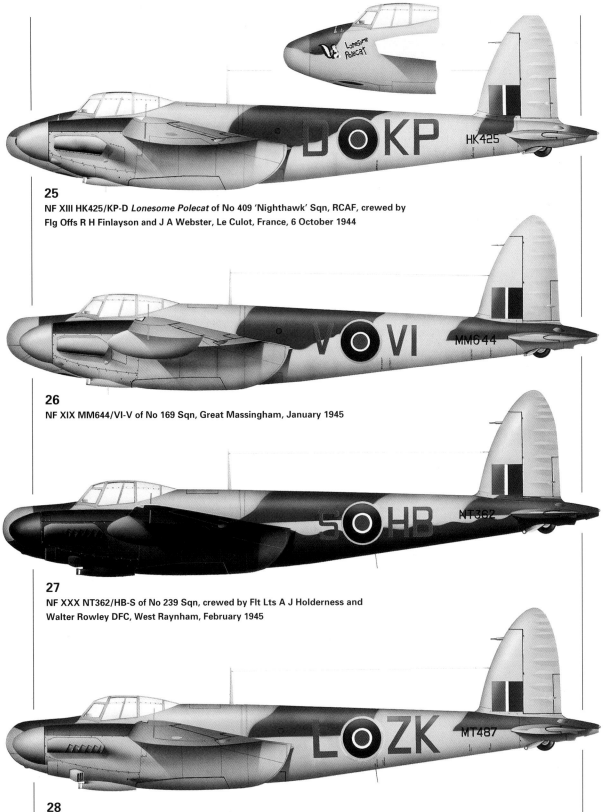

25
NF XIII HK425/KP-D *Lonesome Polecat* of No 409 'Nighthawk' Sqn, RCAF, crewed by
Flg Offs R H Finlayson and J A Webster, Le Culot, France, 6 October 1944

26
NF XIX MM644/VI-V of No 169 Sqn, Great Massingham, January 1945

27
NF XXX NT362/HB-S of No 239 Sqn, crewed by Flt Lts A J Holderness and
Walter Rowley DFC, West Raynham, February 1945

28
NF XXX MT487/ZK-L of No 25 Sqn, Castle Camps, November 1944

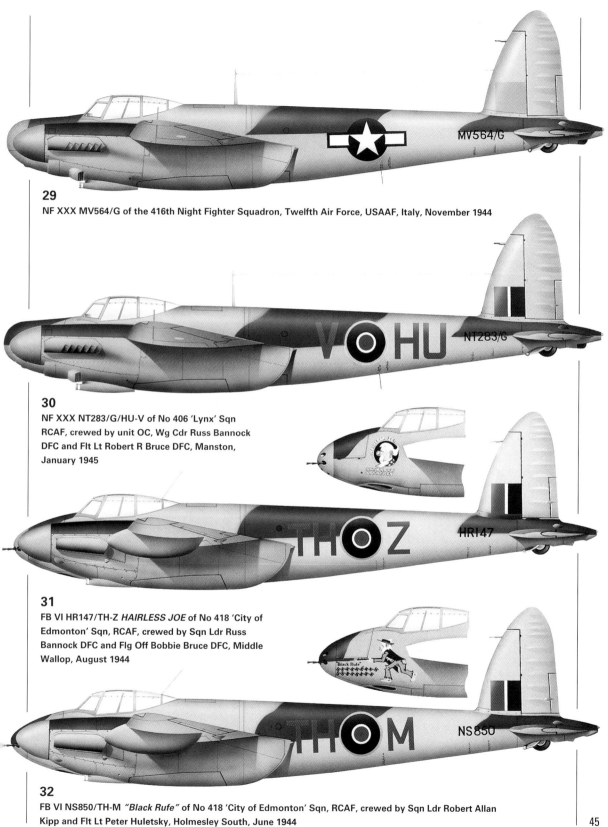

29
NF XXX MV564/G of the 416th Night Fighter Squadron, Twelfth Air Force, USAAF, Italy, November 1944

30
NF XXX NT283/G/HU-V of No 406 'Lynx' Sqn
RCAF, crewed by unit OC, Wg Cdr Russ Bannock
DFC and Flt Lt Robert R Bruce DFC, Manston,
January 1945

31
FB VI HR147/TH-Z *HAIRLESS JOE* of No 418 'City of
Edmonton' Sqn, RCAF, crewed by Sqn Ldr Russ
Bannock DFC and Flg Off Bobbie Bruce DFC, Middle
Wallop, August 1944

32
FB VI NS850/TH-M *"Black Rufe"* of No 418 'City of Edmonton' Sqn, RCAF, crewed by Sqn Ldr Robert Allan
Kipp and Flt Lt Peter Huletsky, Holmesley South, June 1944

1
Flt Lt Ted Cox, 'A' Flight No 29 Sqn,
Ford, February 1944

2
Wg Cdr 'Bob' Braham DSO*, DFC*,
Wing Commander Night Operations
2 Group, 2nd TAF, March 1944

3
Wg Cdr John Cunningham, DSO*,
DFC*, OC No 85 Sqn, West Malling,
September 1943

4
Flt Lt Gordon 'Peter' Panitz DFC,
RAAF, No 456 Sqn, RAAF,
Predannack, June 1943

5
Flg Off R S 'Dickie' Williams, RAAF,
No 456 Sqn, RAAF, Predannack, June
1943

6
Wg Cdr V J 'Pop' Wheeler, DFC*,
MC*, Order of St Stanislaus, OC No
157 Sqn, Bradwell Bay, April 1943

INTRUDING

During the early months of 1944 the main work undertaken by 2nd TAF Mosquito units comprised Day Ranger sorties over France. One of the primary proponents of this type of operation was No 418 Sqn, which had flown its first FB VI mission as long ago as 7 May 1943. By the end of the year the unit was performing

both Intruder and Day Ranger sorties over France and the Low Countries, as Flg Off Bernard Job, Flg Off Jack Phillips' navigator, recalls;

'Being one of the pioneers in Intruder operations, the squadron worked at perfecting techniques aimed at surprising and intercepting enemy aircraft over their own airfields at night, and generally disrupting airfield activity. Given opportunity, ground targets were strafed. The absence of AI equipment in the aircraft plainly made the task of interception much more challenging, but, as results showed, hardly impossible, given the acute observation and perseverance demonstrated by crews.

'What made this type of offensive operation so different from many others was that having been assigned designated patrol areas – often a group of airfields in France or Germany – crews were then free to plan their own routes to and from these areas. Intruder aircraft almost always flew at low altitude, firstly in order to avoid unwanted enemy radar detection, but also to arrive on target at something like aerodrome circuit height. There were, of course, variations on the theme of night intruder patrols. One of these was the Ranger, whereby a single Mosquito penetrated free-lance deep into enemy territory, even as far as Poland and southern Bavaria, Later, Day Rangers took place, usually by pairs of aircraft surprising and destroying enemy aircraft both in the air and on the ground, far afield. The Baltic states became a favourite run, thereby exploiting the Mosquito's long endurance at low speed.'

FB VI HJ821/TH-W of No 418 'City of Edmonton' Sqn, RCAF is seen approaching Ford at the end of a night sortie in early 1944. The Canadians flew their first FB VI operation on 7 May 1943, and by the end of the year they were flying Intruder and Day Ranger operations over France and the Low Countries. This particular Mosquito was a veteran of countless forays across occupied Europe, serving exclusively with No 418 Sqn during its lengthy career in the frontline (*via Tom Cushing*)

On the night of 24 April 1945 Plt Offs L E Fitchett and A C Hardy of No 409 'Nighthawk' Sqn, RCAF destroyed a Ju 52, but upon their return to B108 Rheine just as dawn was breaking, they were struck by fire from another aircraft and their port engine set alight. The attacker overshot, and Hardy quickly recognised it as another Mosquito from an Intruder squadron in the UK before Fitchett carried out an emergency crash-landing. That afternoon the OC of the Intruder squadron in question flew over to Rheine to apologise. Fitchett later lost his life flying Beaufighters with the embryonic Israeli air force during the Jewish state's first war with Egypt in 1948. Hardy, on the other hand, became a professor of architecture at Manchester University (*Ross Finlayson*)

FB VI NS850 *"Black Rufe"* of No 418 Sqn was flown by Sqn Ldr Robert Allan Kipp and Flt Lt Peter Huletsky. As this impressive scoreboard shows, Kipp and Huletsky realised great success during 1943-45, claiming ten aircraft shot down and one shared destroyed, one shared probable, one damaged, seven destroyed on the ground and eight damaged on the ground – the bulk of these were scored between December 1943 and June 1944 in this aircraft. NS850 was written off in a landing accident at Hunsdon on 1 November 1944 when the fighter overshot the runway following an air test, its pilot having been forced to recover back at the Hertfordshire base with an engine feathered (*Stephen M Fochuk*)

On 27 January 1944 Flt Lt James Johnson RCAF, with Plt Off John Caine, and Plt Off Earl Boal used their FB VIs to attack Clermont-Ferrand airfield. Johnson downed a Ju 88 and damaged a Ju 86, plus shared in the destruction of two Junkers W 34s with Caine, who also destroyed a Ju 88. By 8 May, John Caine had destroyed 12 aircraft on the ground or on water, as well as having damaged five more – later, in April-May 1945, Caine, now with No 406 Sqn flying NF XXXs, continued his destructive ways by destroying a Ju 88 on the ground and damaging four others.

On 21 March American pilot Lt James F Luma, with Flg Off Colin Finlayson, and Flt Lt Donald MacFadyen and 'Pinky' Wright (all No 418 Sqn crews) flew a long-range Ranger over France. Luma and Finlayson attacked Luxeuil airfield, where they shot down a W 34 liaison aircraft and a Ju 52/3m, and damaged two Gotha Go 242 glider transports and two Bf 109s on the ground, while MacFadyen and Wright downed a Bv 141 which was coming into land. Moving on to Hagenau airfield, MacFadyen proceeded to destroy nine Go 242s and a Do 217 on the ground – he later operated with No 406 Sqn, flying NF XXXs on night Intruders and finishing the war with seven aircraft and five V1s destroyed, plus five aircraft destroyed and seventeen damaged on the ground. Luma finished his tour in April and was awarded both a British and American DFC.

With the formation of the 2nd Tactical Air Force in June 1943, greater emphasis was placed on the offensive capabilities of the FB VI nigh fighter squadrons. Indeed, by early 1944 their main contribution towards the eventual Allied victory in Europe was being performed on Day Ranger operations over France

Although Day Rangers were the 'bread and butter' of 2nd TAF's Mosquito fighter units by the spring of 1944, the versatility of the FB VI allowed these self-same squadrons to also perform night intruder sorties as a matter of routine. Here, a Mosquito taxies out from its dispersal for a night intruder sortie over occupied Europe bathed in white light for the attendant press – ideal for cameras but hardly conducive conditions for the crew to attain effective night vision (*via Tom Cushing*)

Thirty-one-year-old Wg Cdr Robert Carl 'Moose' Fumerton DFC*, from Fort Coulonge, Quebec, destroyed 14 enemy aircraft (12 of them defending Malta flying Beaufighters with No 89 Sqn in 1942). Prior to his posting to the Mediterranean, Fumerton had claimed the first RCAF night victory of the war (a Ju 88) flying Beaufighter IIF R2336 with No 406 'Lynx' Sqn on 1/2 September 1942. In August 1943 he was given command of his old unit, and he duly scored his 14th victory (again a Ju 88 – no less than eight of his fourteen kills were over Junkers 'twins') with the 'Lynx' squadron on 14/15 May 1944 in a Mosquito NF XII south-east of Portland, in Dorset. 'Moose' was to lead No 406 Sqn until July 1944, and he finished the war as the top-scoring Canadian nightfighter ace with 14 destroyed and one damaged (*Stephen M Fochuk*)

On 14 April Sqn Ldr Robert Kipp and Flt Lt Pete Huletsky, also of No 418 Sqn, downed two Ju 52/3m minesweepers fitted with de-gaussing rings and destroyed two Do 217s on the ground and damaged a third. Kipp's final tally included ten aircraft shot down and seven destroyed and eight damaged on the ground. Meanwhile, Stan Cotterill and 'Pop' McKenna claimed four in a single night sortie, whilst Australian Sqn Ldr Charlie Scherf racked up 23 destroyed (13 in the air) in just four months between 27 January and 16 May 1944.

In fact, during April-May 1944, No 418 Sqn shot down 30 enemy aircraft in the air and destroyed a further 38 on the ground. The unit scored their 100th victory in May, and in June flew anti-Diver patrols at night, before reverting in September to Rangers and abortive 'Big Ben' patrols (trying to 'jam' V2 rockets). No 418 Sqn finished the war with the distinction of having destroyed more aircraft, both in the air and on the ground, than any other RCAF unit in either night or daylight operations.

In the spring of 1944, Nos 29, 264, 409, 410, 488 and 604 Sqns, equipped with either NF XIIs or XIIIs, formed No 85 (Base) Group for the purpose of providing fighter cover leading up to, and in the wake of, D-Day. On 5/6 June, 2nd TAF's Mosquito fighter units performed defensive operations (No 264 Sqn had actually flown jamming patrols

before they went looking for fighters) over the invasion coast. They also performed a secondary role, as Bernard Job of No 418 Sqn recalls;

'The squadron was stationed at Holmesley South, near Bournemouth, and six aircrews were detailed to act as "flak bait" to cover the paratroop and glider drops in the Cherbourg Peninsular by drawing searchlights and flak away from these more vulnerable aircraft. So successful was this that two of the six were hit, one so badly that it crash landed near base and burnt up. The crew ran for their lives!'

Luftwaffe activity on 5/6 June was almost non-existent. Less than 50 plots were made, and only Flg Off R E Lelong RNZAF and Plt Off J A McLaren in a No 605 Sqn FB VI scored a kill when they destroyed an Me 410 seven miles south-east of Evreux airfield – Flg Offs Pearce and Moore of No 409 Sqn also claimed a probable in an NF XIII.

The following night Flt Lt Allison and Flg Off Stanton of No 29 Sqn destroyed a Ju 52/3m and a UEA over Coulommiers airfield, whilst a second Junkers transport was claimed by No 418 Sqn FB VI crew Flt Lts Don MacFadyen DFC, RCAF and 'Pinky' Wright in HR155 north of the airfield. Flt Lt E L Williams DFC of No 605 Sqn also used an FB VI to down a Ju 88 over Orleans-Bricy airfield, and Mosquito ace Wg Cdr K M Hampshire, OC of No 456 RAAF, and Flt Lt T Condon destroyed a He 177 three miles east of Barfleur in NF XVII HK286.

On 7/8 June Mosquito nightfighters downed eight aircraft over France, No 456 Sqn claiming four He 177s within this total. Twenty-fours later Flt Lt J C I Hooper DFC and Flg Off Hubbard DFM of No 604 Sqn used NF XIII MM500 to destroy a Bf 110 north-east of Laval, and Flg Off Wigglesworth and Sgt Blomfield of No 29 Sqn claimed a Ju 88. On the night of the 9th/10th, the latter unit 'bagged' two more enemy aircraft, whilst No 456 Sqn shot down yet another He 177 and a Do 217 – on 5 July the Australians claimed three aircraft to bring the unit's score to 30 victories since 1 March. In addition, two Ju 188s were destroyed by

On 5 March 1944 Wg Cdr John Randall Daniel 'Bob' Braham DSO, DFC*, Wing Commander Night Operations at HQ, No 2 Group, 2nd TAF, scored his 21st victory of the war, and his first on Mosquitoes. Flying FB VI LR364/SY-E, borrowed from No 613 'City of Manchester' Sqn, with Flt Lt W J 'Sticks' Gregory DFC, DFM, Braham downed He 177 SJ+RL of 3./KG 100 near Chateaudun. Very much an outspoken individualist, unsurpassed in his sheer aggressive fighting spirit and relentless determination, Braham, was eventually shot down by Lt Robert Spreckels of JG 1 on 25 June 1944 during a Day Ranger to Denmark in a No 21 Sqn FB VI and made a PoW. His final wartime tally of 29 victories included nine scored with the FB VI (*IWM*)

No 418 Sqn crews pose for the camera in front of a well-worn FB VI. American Lt James F Luma, is seen seventh from left in his distinctive USAAF uniform. On 21 March 1944 Luma and Flg Off Colin Finlayson downed a W34 liaison aircraft and a Ju 52/3m transport, as well as damaging two Gotha Go 242 glider transports and two Bf 109s on the ground at Luxeuil airfield (*Tom Cushing*)

Although this photo was specially staged and lit for the cameraman, it nonetheless shows the formidable fire-power of four machine guns and four cannon available to FB VI crews (*via Tom Cushing*)

NF XIII HK425/KP-D *Lonesome Polecat* of No 409 'Nighthawk' Sqn, RCAF is seen parked on the unit's grass dispersal at Twente, in Holland. On 25/26 November 1944 Flg Off R I E Britten RCAF and Flt Lt L E Fownes shot down a Ju 88 and damaged a second Junkers bomber over at Rheindahlen in this aircraft – by war's end this pairing had destroyed five aircraft. HK425 had previously served with No 96 Sqn prior to being transferred to the Canadian unit, with whom it remained until the squadron was disbanded on 1 July 1945. After spending five months in storage, the veteran nightfighter was stuck off charge on 21 November 1945 (*Ross Finlayson*)

Flg Offs Al Webster and Ross H Finlayson also flew *Lonesome Polecat* during their tour with No 409 'Nighthawk' Sqn (*RCAF*)

Nos 409 and 410 Sqns that same night. On 14/15 June Russ Bannock and Bob Bruce of No 418 Sqn achieved their first victory just a week after joining the unit. Bruce recalls;

'Our first Intruder was a two-hour patrol off Bourges-Avord airfield. Luck was with us, and after some time we spotted the exhaust of a night-fighter as it passed overhead. We picked it up as it turned on final approach, but had to break off to the south due to heavy AA fire. Fortunately for us the pilot switched on his landing lights. We attacked in a shallow dive and fired a burst of cannon and machine guns. As it exploded and caught fire, we recognised it as a Bf 110. We were subjected to a barrage from the north side of the airfield, and we turned sharply to the left to avoid this wall of fire, but Russ was reefing so hard on the elevator that we did a high-speed stall just as we almost turned 190°. The aircraft flick-rolled to the right and Russ caught it after we rolled almost 180°. We then exited to the west of the field. We were, by the way, still carrying two bombs under the wings, and by the time we reached Holmesley South, our fuel reserves were getting low. It was a memorable first trip.'

By the end of June the nightfighters and fighter-bombers of 85 Base Group had destroyed 76 aircraft and claimed five probables. In July the six squadrons downed 55 aircraft and claimed two probables. In addition, Bradwell Bay-based NF XVIIs of No 219 Sqn within Fighter Command

Feldwebel Robert Koch's Bf 110 G9+MN of 5./NJG 1 explodes near Peer, Belgium, at about 2320 hours on 7 October 1944 as a result of Flg Offs Ross Finlayson and Al Webster's attack in NF XIII MM560. In the minutes prior to this interception, Koch had made a 180° turn to port and set course for his base at Düsseldorf, totally unaware that the Canadian nightfighter had been alerted to his presence by Allied GCI. The NF XIII crew approached unobserved from astern, the GCI controller bringing them in to visual range because the Mosquito's radar had gone 'wonky'. Once close enough to see the contact, it was discovered that the enemy aircraft boasted external wing tanks, leading Finlayson to believe that his target was a four-engined aircraft. He therefore misjudged the closing speed and distance between himself and the Bf 110, scoring hits in the port wing and fuselage with his first burst but ending up right below the Messerschmitt with his wheels and flaps extended. However, before Koch had time to take evasive action, a second burst was fired which rendered the Bf 110's controls useless and set the port wing alight, whereupon the pilot, who was flying his 70th operation, gave the order to bale out. Koch was slightly injured whilst taking to his parachute, but his bordfunker, Unteroffizier Heinz Forster, and gunner, Unteroffizier Ernst Darg, were both killed. Robert Koch, who had five four-engined RAF bombers to his credit (scored between February and August 1944), had previously been shot down during a daylight mission on 14 October 1943 by a USAAF P-47 shortly after joining 6./NJG 1. He did not fly again until February 1944, and in August joined 5./NJG 1. A highly experienced Bf 110 pilot, Koch had also flown with ZG 2 in Russia, NJG 5 at Stendal and 7./NJG 1 at Twente (*Ross Finlayson*)

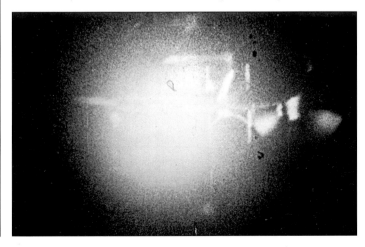

NF XIII MM560 of No 409 'Nighthawk' Sqn is seen at Le Culot, in Belgium, on the morning of 7 October 1944 following Finlayson and Webster's shooting down of Koch's Bf 110. MM560 was normally flown by Sqn Ldr Hatch, OC 'A' Flight, but as the two Canadians had no aircraft of their own, they would take any Mosquito that was serviceable. This aircraft remained with the Canadians until written off in a belly landing at Lille/Vendeville on 13 March 1945 – the Mosquito's undercarriage had jammed during an air test. The NF XXX parked in the distance behind MM560 is the No 410 Sqn aircraft in which Flt Lts Ben Plummer DFC and Hargrove had been vectored onto a second Bf 110 the previous night and lost an engine to return fire. Plummer weaved to dodge the German's bullets and the Bf 110 pilot lost control and crashed (*Ross Finlayson*)

had shot down six Ju 88/188s either over, or in the vicinity of, the beach-head – Flg Off D T Tull had got two of them. No 219 Sqn eventually joined No 147 Wing, 85 (Base) Group, 2nd TAF on 28 August.

On 6 August No 604 Sqn at Zeals (which had joined No 141 Wing, 2nd TAF, in April, transferring to No 147 Wing, No 85 (Base) Group, on 3 May) became the first Mosquito fighter squadron to move to France, when it transferred to A8 at Picauville. That month, 77 aircraft were destroyed in the air by the seven nightfighter and fighter-bomber squadrons – No 418 Sqn also destroyed aircraft on the ground. On the night of the 29/30 August, Russ Bannock and Bob Bruce, paired with Californian Flg Off Sid Seid and Dave McIntosh, blew up a Ju 88 on the ground at Copenhagen-Kastrup and a Bf 110 at Vaerose airfield. Seid, who scored hits on a line of three aircraft, observed a mechanic working around the tail section of the Bf 110 as they approached.

'After one look at us', Seid recalled, 'the "Erk" broke all speed records during a sprint in an easterly direction. During my attack, another "Erk" was observed descending a high ladder near the roof of a hangar. Upon seeing us the speed of his descent was suddenly, and forcibly, increased by

NF XIII HK415/KP-R of No 409 Sqn is seen getting its acceptance check on arrival at Lille airfield in November 1944. Note that the hangars in the background behind the Spitfire have been camouflaged as farm buildings. On 18/19 December 1944 Flg Off's Webster and Finlayson destroyed a Ju 88 in this aircraft, which was lost in a take-off accident at the airfield on 18 January 1945 (*Ross Finlayson*)

a backward fall from near the top of the ladder. I claim this "Erk" as "probably destroyed".'

Victories in September and October failed to match the numbers scored in June and July, however, although the nightfighters nevertheless maintained a credible response. During September they destroyed 28 aircraft of many types, followed in October by a further 15. On 21 November, No 136 Wing was created within 2nd TAF with the arrival of ex-Fighter Command units Nos 418 and 605 Sqns at Hartford Bridge. That month 14 aircraft fell to 2nd TAF Mosquito nightfighters.

Weather and drastically reduced enemy activity saw successes become extremely hard to come by in December 1944. Indeed, only three Ju 88s and two Bf 110s were destroyed between the 4th and the 18th/19th. The latter success fell to Wg Cdr James D Somerville DFC, OC of No 409 Sqn, who scored his sixth confirmed victory in NF XIII MM456 with Flg Off G D Robinson DFC when they despatched a Ju 88 in the Kaiserworth area. Flt Lt C E Edinger RCAF and Flg Off C C Vaessen of No 410 Sqn, also gained a kill on this night in NF XXX MV527 when they shot down a Ju 88 south of Bonninghardt.

NF XXX MM767 of No 410 'Cougar' Sqn rests on PSP (Pierced Steel Planking) in a muddy dispersal at either B48/Glisy or B51 Lille-Vendeville in the winter of 1944/45. On 29/30 October 1944 Lt A A Harrington, USAAF and Flg Off D G Tongue shot down a Fw 190 whilst flying this aircraft in the Venlo area. On 25/26 November this crew, again in MM767, destroyed three Ju 88Gs at Muntz, Jacberath and north of Hunxe, thus raising their final tally to seven. MM767 survived the war and subsequently became one of 23 surplus RAF NF 30s passed to the *Armée de l'Air* in February 1948 (*Stephen M Fochuk*)

This ground firing test by an FB VI graphically illustrates the awesome, and concentrated, firepower of the Mosquito intruder (*via Les Bulmer*)

Christmas drew near, and 2nd TAF enjoyed a very eventful Yuletide. On the night of 22/23 December, No 219 Sqn's OC, Wg Cdr Peter Green DSO, DFC, and Flt Lt Oxby DFM** used NF XXX MM792 to destroy a Ju 88, followed by a second Junkers bomber south of Huy 24 hours later. A further two crews from No 219 Sqn also destroyed a pair of Ju 88s on this night.

The following night, 2nd TAF NF XXX and XIII crews enjoyed further successes when they downed no fewer than ten enemy aircraft. Flt Lt McPhail and Flg Off Donaghue of No 409 Sqn destroyed a Ju 188 and Flg Offs Mackenzie and Bodard of No 410 Sqn claimed two Ju 88s, whilst four more aircraft fell to crews from No 488 Sqn, RNZAF, based at B48/Amiens-Glisy. The kills for the latter unit were split between squadron OC, Wg Cdr R G Watts, and Flg Off I C Skudder, who got a Ju 188, Flt Lt Johnny Hall DFC and Flg Off J P W Cairns DFC with an Me 410 in the US Sector and Flt Lt Kenneth W 'Chunky' Stewart (a solidly built, 5 ft 2 in, solicitor from Dunedin) and Flg Off H E 'Bill' Brumby, who claimed two Ju 88s in NF XXX MM822. It was the latter crew's first encounter with the enemy, as Stewart relates;

'While on patrol near Roermond I noticed clusters of white flares and obtained permission to investigate. The controller said that there was no activity in that direction, but Bill Brumby succeeded in putting me on to an aircraft. After a short chase, with the target taking mild evasive action, we both identified the objective as a Ju 88, but for positive identification, I closed to 100 ft, whereupon the enemy aircraft fired off a red flare which illuminated the black crosses on the fin, fuselage and mainplane. I dropped back to 150 yards and fired a short burst. Strikes were observed

The squadrons of 85 (Base) Group helped provide fighter cover leading up to, during and after D-Day. For example, on 5/6 June 2nd TAF's Mosquito fighter squadrons performed defensive operations (No 264 Sqn actually flew radar-jamming patrols before they went looking for enemy fighters) over the invasion coast. This aircraft is seen having its distinctive full-size AEAF (Allied Expeditionary Air Force) *Overlord* invasion stripes applied at an airfield somewhere in southern England just prior to D-Day. By September 1944 the stripes were carried around the fuselage only, and by December their presence had been reduced further to just the lower mid- to rear-fuselage section (*via Harry Wilson*)

No 418 Sqn's then Sqn Ldr Paul Y Davoud DSO, DFC (pointing) and his navigator, Flt Lt Douglas Alcorn DFC (above), are seen with Sqn Ldr C C Moran DFC during a debriefing session held in the wake of a successful intruder operation. On 27/28 June 1943 Sqn Ldr Moran had claimed a Ju 88 and an He 111 destroyed at Avord, the pilot also blasting a train and a radio mast during the same sortie. By the end of the summer he had earned a deserved reputation as a 'train-buster', his technique usually consisting of a strafing run to stop the locomotive, before finishing it off with bombs. Having attained wing commander rank, Paul Davoud led the squadron from June 1943 through to January 1944 (*Stephen M Fochuk*)

A native of Montreal, Donald Aikins MacFadyen joined the RCAF in May 1940. His first score came whilst flying FB VIs with No 418 Sqn when he was awarded a 'probable' on 22/23 December 1943 against a UEA. MacFadyen followed this up in early 1944 with the destruction of an Me 410, a Ju 52/3m and five V1s. Aside from his aerial successes, MacFadyen also exploited the FB VI's (in this case MM426) excellent ground strafing capabilities, which included a haul on 21 March 1944 of eight Go 242s damaged and a ninth destroyed, along with a Do 217, during a long-range Day Ranger to Hagenau airfield, in France. Flt Lt MacFadyen, accompanied by Flt Lt 'Pinky' Wright, had also shot down a Bv 131 attempting to land at Luxeuil airfield prior to attacking Hagenau. Promoted to squadron leader, MacFadyen joined No 406 'Lynx' Sqn in November 1944, where he flew the NF XXX on night Intruders. He was awarded a DFC and bar, an American DFC and the DSO during his two tours, and he finished the war with a tally of seven aircraft and five V1s destroyed in the air, and five aircraft destroyed, one probable and seventeen damaged on the ground (*Stephen M Fochuk*)

between the port engine and fuselage. With a second burst the port engine caught fire and the Hun spun down in flames, exploding before hitting the ground ten miles west of Maeseyck.

'The controller told me to climb to 7000 ft, and whilst doing so I saw further flares and again requested permission to chase. After changing controllers, Bill Brumby seized the opportunity and, after the enemy aircraft had throttled back, turned, climbed and straightened out, I obtained a visual at 2000 ft which Bill confirmed with his glasses as another Ju 88. At 300 yards this aircraft also dropped reddish flares and we plainly saw black crosses and also the bomb racks. I closed in to 200-150 yards and gave two short bursts, which started a fire in the fuselage. The enemy did a diving turn to starboard and when I was down to 1000 ft, he hit the ground and exploded.'

On 24/25 December a dozen

Flg Off Sid Seid DFC of No 418 Sqn is seen leaning out of the cockpit of his FB VI TH-J, with his dog 'Mostitch' and Flt Lt Tommy Mathew sat alongside him on the wing. Seid, an American-Jew from California who enlisted in the RCAF, was hell bent on destroying the Nazis, and would apparently stop at nothing to get at them. Sid's usual navigator was Flg Off Dave McIntosh DFC, who, postwar, wrote a book entitled *Terror in the Starboard Seat* about his experiences flying with Sid Seid. The emblem seen painted on the cockpit access door was an unofficial No 418 Sqn crest (*Stephen M Fochuk*)

more enemy aircraft were shot down by 2nd TAF Mosquito nightfighter units, which had despatched 139 aircraft on Christmas Eve to targets in south-west Germany. One of the units involved was No 410 Sqn, which sent off nine NF XXXs on frontline patrols between 1750 hours on Christmas Eve and 0530 hours on Christmas Day. Whilst orbiting the Wassemberg area in NF XXX MV527, Flt Lt C E Edinger DFC and Flg Off C C Vaessen DFC destroyed a Ju 87 from *Nachtschlachtgruppe* 1 (used for harassment of troops and transport – see *Osprey Combat Aircraft 6 - Ju 87 Stukageschwader of the Mediterranean and North Africa* for further details) and a second fell to Sqn Ldr I E MacTavish and Flg Off A M Grant in NF XXX MT485. Squadronmates Flg Off J A Watt and Flt Lt E H Collis also tasted success over the Roermond-Julich area when they claimed a Ju 88 of 2./NJG 2. The bomber crashed near Roermond, killing pilot Tetzlaff and leaving the remaining three crewmen as PoWs.

Another victorious crew on Christmas Eve was that of Flt Lt G R I Parker DFC, DSM and Wt Off D L Godfrey DFC, DFM of No 219 Sqn, who used NF XXX MM698 to destroy a Ju 188 12 miles east of Eindhoven, followed by a second Junkers 'twin' 34 miles east of Arnhem.

Wg Cdr Russ Bannock DFC*, who was now OC No 406 Sqn, obtained his sixth kill on this night flying NF XXX MM693, his victim (Ju 88G-1 Wk-Nr 714132 3C+CT of 9./NJG 4) crashing ten kilometres west of Paderborn – both crewmen, Oberfeldwebel Manfred Ludwig and Feldwebel Hans Fischl, were killed.

No 604 Sqn's Flt Lts R J Foster DFC and M F Newton DFC also claimed a probable kill east of Nijmegen on the 24th/25th whilst flying NF XIII MM462 from Odiham, although their foe was not a vulnerable bomber, but rather a potentially deadly He 219 nightfighter. Flt Lts

Stephenson and Hall of No 219 Sqn also encountered a nightfighter in the form of a Bf 110, which they duly despatched.

Despite rising losses of experienced crews and fuel deprivation, the Luftwaffe's nightfighter force still posed a considerable threat to Bomber Command. However, on 1 January 1945 it was the turn of their day fighter colleagues to take the fight to the Allies *en masse* when the *Jagdwaffe* attempted one last major air offensive on the continent, codenamed Operation *Bodenplatte*. Preparations for the attack had commenced on 20 December 1944,

Flt Lt Jack H Phillips DFC, RCAF and his navigator, Flg Off Bernard M Job RAFVR (sat on the wing) were also part of No 418 Sqn. They are seen here posing for the camera on FB VI NT137/TH-T *Lady Luck* at Hartfordbridge in February 1945. The Canadian squadron moved to Coxyde (B71) in March 1945 in order to fly operations on the continent. A considerable number of RCAF-manned Mosquitoes appear to have carried nose art either on the aircraft itself or, as in this case, on the removable crew cockpit access hatch (*Bernard M Job*)

when the first *Jagdgeschwader* had been transferred to airfields in the west from the Eastern Front. By New Year's Day, near on 1000 fighters had been massed in western Germany, and at 0745 hours that Sunday morning, around 850 fighters took off and attacked 27 airfields in northern France, Belgium and southern Holland. The four-hour operation succeeded in destroying about 100 Allied aircraft, but in turn cost the Luftwaffe 300 aircraft, most of which were shot down by anti-aircraft guns deployed primarily to defend against possible V1 attacks.

One aircraft which escaped the bombing at Brussels was an NF XXX flown in by 'Chunky' Stewart which had been shot up the night before following an enemy aircraft on approach to the German nightfighter base at Rheine. With its hydraulics shot away, the Mosquito had careered off the runway with a collapsed undercarriage. Following its removal from the runway, the fighter had been 'tucked' under the wing of a Flying Fortress for the night, which had in turn sheltered it from the worst of the attacking fire rained on the airfield just hours later.

No 418 Sqn's FB VI HR147 was dubbed *HAIRLESS JOE* by its crew, Sqn Ldr Russ Bannock DFC (above, left – he later became a wing commander and squadron OC, receiving a DSO and DFC*) and his navigator, Flg Off Bobbie Bruce DFC. Both of these photographs were taken at Middle Wallop in August 1944. No 418 Sqn ended the war as the top scoring Canadian fighter unit, period, both in respect to the number of aircraft destroyed in the air and on the ground (*Bernard M Job*)

On 1/2 January 2nd TAF Mosquitoes exacted a measure of revenge when No 604 Sqn's Flt Lts R J Foster DFC and M F Newton DFC downed a trio of Ju 88s. By the end of the month, 2nd TAF Mosquito nightfighters had shot down 17 aircraft, including, on 23/24 January, two Ju 88s by No 409 Sqn NF XIIIs. These particular aircraft had been Ju 88S-3s of 1./KG 66 and *Lehrgeschwader* 1, tasked with bombing and mining river traffic in the Scheldt estuary in an attempt to prevent supplies reaching Antwerp. Plt Offs M G Kent and Simpson used NF XIII MM466 to down an LG 1 Ju 88 over the mouth of the Scheldt, this aircraft being just one of three lost by the unit that night. Amongst the Ju 88s lost that night were the aircraft flown by *Gruppenkommandeur*, Hauptmann Hecking (Wk-Nr 301348 L1+GK), and 6./LG 1's *Staffelführer*, Oberleutnant Huber (Wk-Nr 331294 L1+NP).

While there is some doubt about which LG 1 aircraft fell to Kent and Simpson, there is no question that the Ju 188E-1 shot down three miles west of Dienst that same night by squadron OC, Wg Cdr James D Somerville DFC, and Plt Off A C Hardy in NF XIII MM456 was Wk-Nr 260542 A3+QD, flown by Obergefreiter Heinz Hauck, who was on a clandestine mission for KG 200's *Kommando Olga*. Hauck had taken off from Rhein-Main and successfully dropped two agents near Gilze-Rijen, in the liberated part of Holland, before heavy AA bursts and searchlights had given away his position to the 'Nighthawk' crew, who were returning from patrol at 8000 ft. Somerville and Hardy were directed by 'Rejoice' (a GCI station) towards the 'bogey', which was six miles away from them at 4000 ft. Somerville reduced height and Hardy was further assisted by

Two FB VI crews study a map of the continent for the benefit of the attendant press photographer prior to manning their respective aircraft. Shoes rather than boots, and uniforms instead of fleece-lined jackets, were normally worn by Mosquito aircrew because the heat produced by the two Merlin engines 'flying in line-abreast formation close by' quickly made the aircraft's small cockpit unbearably hot (*via Mick Jennings*)

Hailing from Belt, Montana, Lt James Forrest Luma DFC joined the RCAF in 1941. He was then transferred to the USAAF in July 1943, but flew a tour with No 418 Sqn in order to gain valuable nightfighting experience with the Mosquito. Lt Luma is seen here with his regular navigator, Flg Off Colin Finlayson (closest to the camera), inspecting damage to the rudder of their Mosquito. On 21 March 1944 the pair downed a W34 and a Ju 52/3m, as well as damaging two Go 242 glider transports and two Bf 109s on the ground at Luxeuil airfield. Luma, who finished his tour in April 1944, and was awarded both a British and American DFC, scored seven destroyed and two damaged in the air, and four damaged on the ground, during his time with the RCAF (*Stephen M Fochuk*)

FB VI *Moonbeam McSwine* of No 418 Sqn was flown by Lt Luma (smoking the pipe) and navigator Flg Off Finlayson (right). Wg Cdr 'Howie' Cleveland (far left) and his navigator, Flt Sgt Frank Day DFM (middle), are the remaining aircrew seen in this photo (*Stephen M Fochuk*)

'Bricktile' and then 'Laundry' GCI stations until they came upon the Ju 188E-1, which had reduced its height to 3000 ft. Hardy had difficulty keeping his quarry out of the ground clutter on his AI Mk VIII scope at their height of 2500 ft until he finally secured a solid contact at two miles. Somerville then closed to 1500 ft for a positive identification. Satisfied that it was indeed a Ju 188, he closed still further and opened fire with his cannons at a distance of just 200 ft. His first burst set fire to Hauck's port engine, the 20 mm shells causing a brilliant explosion which forced the Mosquito pilot, who had been momentarily blinded, to break away.

Somerville came in again for a second firing pass as Hauck desperately

Sqn Ldr David John 'Blackie' Williams DFC (left) and his navigator, Flg Off C J Kirkpatrick, are seen in front of their No 406 Sqn Mosquito, which was aptly named *"Blackie" & "Kirk"*. Williams, a native of Vancouver, joined the RCAF in 1940 and began his tour flying Hampdens with No 408 Sqn. Perhaps his most notable achievement with the Handley Page bomber came on 27/28 August 1942 during a night raid on Kassel when he shot down a Ju 88 with the fixed pilot's gun, and then repulsed an attack by a Bf 109 on the return flight home. Flt Lt Williams was awarded a DFC soon after this sortie, and he went on to complete his tour the following October. Following a spell with No 410 Sqn as a flight commander and conversion onto fighters at No 54 OTU, 'Blackie' was promoted to squadron leader in August 1943 and posted to No 406 'Lynx' Sqn as a flight commander. He subsequently attained wing commander rank in July 1944 and was given command of the unit. By this time he had shot down a He 177 whilst flying a Beaufighter, two Do 217s on 29/30 April flying a Mosquito NF XII and 1½ Do 217s in NF XXX MM731 during a Day Ranger on 21 July – the half took the form of a Do 217 that he had hit in one engine and set alight before he had broken off as the crew were baling out, only for another Mosquito to cut in, fire, and claim the credit for shooting it down! Williams was awarded a DSO in September 1944 and finished the war with five and one shared destroyed (*Stephen M Fochuk*)

"Blackie" & "Kirk."

dived and stall turned in a vain attempt to extinguish the flames. The Canadian's second burst missed, but his third ripped the Ju 188's port wingtip off and the enemy aircraft dived steeply into the ground, giving Somerville his seventh, and final, victory of the war. Hauck, his observer, Gefreiter Kurt Wuttge, bordfunker, Unteroffizier Max Grossman, and despatcher Feldwebel Heinrich Hoppe baled out to become PoWs.

By this stage of the war the Luftwaffe was reeling from the effects of the Allied bombing campaign, particularly in respect to its fuel reserves. This resulted in German night flying activity being restricted to particular nights, with long intervals in between. Victories, therefore, became hard to find, although on 3/4 February No 409 Sqn's Plt Offs Kent and Simpson added to their score with the destruction of a Ju 88, whilst Flt Lts B E Plumer DFC and Hargrove of No 410 Sqn despatched a more formidable foe in the shape of a He 219 Uhu.

On 22 February all 2nd TAF crews and serviceable aircraft were pressed into action for Operation *Clarion*, which was intended to be the 'coup de grace' for the German transport system. Some 9000 aircraft attacked railway stations, trains and engines, crossroads, bridges, ships and barges on canals and rivers, stores and other targets. It was to be the last time that Mosquitoes operated in daylight in such numbers, and losses were high.

Aerial clashes in the night skies over Germany had immediately preceded *Clarion*, and a number of Luftwaffe aircraft were destroyed by 2nd TAF's Mosquitoes. One of those to claim a kill was No 406 Sqn's Flt Lt Don A MacFadyen, who downed a Bf 110 east of Stormede airfield. 'Chunky' Stewart and Bill Brumby in No 488 Sqn NF XXX NT263 also saw action whilst patrolling over Holland, having been alerted by GCI that they were being pursued by an unidentified aircraft. It was a Ju 88G, and in the ensuing dogfight Stewart finally got the upper hand. At last behind the enemy aircraft, he quickly identified it as a Ju 88G and gave the Junkers 'twin' a quick burst of cannon fire using a fairly wide deflection. The machine exploded near Groenlo. Three nights later, on 24/25 February, No 219 Sqn's Wg Cdr Peter Green and Flt Lt D Oxby used NF

XXX MM792 to down a Stuka, whilst on the 28th, Don MacFadyen claimed an UEA 'probably destroyed' at Hailfingen in NF XXX NT325.

March brought more successes for 2nd TAF Mosquito nightfighter units, with Don MacFadyen and NT325 pairing up once again on the 5th/6th to destroy a Ju 88G at Gerolzhofen. On 12/13 March Flt Lt J W Welford and Flg Off R H Phillips of No 410 Sqn claimed a Ju 88 'probable' in the Dunkirk area, while three more victories were recorded on the night of the 21st/22nd – a No 604 Sqn NF XIII crew despatched a Bf 110 in the Dhunn area, and Flg Off R I E Britten DFC, RCAF and Flt Lt L E Fownes DFC of No 409 Sqn claimed a second Messerschmitt 'twin'. The third victory of the night – also a Bf 110 – was claimed by Flg Offs K Fleming and K L Nagle of No 488 Sqn.

Daylight sorties on the 24th saw two crews from No 264 Sqn each destroy a Ju 88, whilst that night three aircraft were downed by No 604 and 410 Sqns. Twenty-four hours later crews from Nos 409, 264 and 219 Sqns despatched two Bf 110s and a pair of Ju 88s, plus one 'probable'.

There was a great deal of activity on 26/27 March, with raids concentrated on the Rhine bridgehead at Emmerich forcing the Luftwaffe into the night sky, but with disastrous results. Flg Offs T R Wood and R Leafe of No 604 Sqn used NF XIII MM497 to down a Ju 88, Flg Offs Reed and Bricker of No 219 Sqn 'bagged' a Ju 188, and Flt Lts B E Plumer DFC and Bradford of No 410 Sqn destroyed a Bf 110. Flt Lt Johnny Hall DFC and Plt Off Taylor of No 488 Sqn (in NF XXX NT314) also destroyed a Ju 88 20 miles north of Emmerich, but in so doing had their fighter damaged by flying debris Hall nursed the Mosquito to Gilze-Rijen, where the aircraft burst into flames as it landed on its belly. Fortunately the canopy's exit panel came away easily, and Hall and Taylor clambered out unhurt.

'Chunky' Stewart and Bill Brumby were also on patrol over the bridgehead that night in NF XXX NT263, and about eight miles north-west of Bocholt they intercepted a Bf 110 which, after a short burst of cannon, hit the ground with a brilliant explosion. Their radar set then became partially inoperable, but Brumby nevertheless managed to pick up a contact, which turned out to be a He 111. Stewart fired twice at the Heinkel and it went into a steep dive. At the same time he realised that he was being chased by a nightfighter, forcing him to break off the engagement.

There were many hours of patient patrolling and sky-searching before Stewart and Brumby added to their score on the night of 7/8 April after being directed onto a 'bogey' over the Ruhr. It was a Bf 110. In the long chase that followed, the rear gunner of the enemy nightfighter opened fire on their NF XXX several times, but Stewart was unable to get his sights on the enemy machine, nor fire his guns. Presently, a small fire started in the tail of the Bf 110 and then grew larger until it dived into the ground and exploded. Although the Mosquito's guns had not been fired, Stewart and Brumby were credited with the destruction of the aircraft – the gunner had shot off his own tail! It was the Kiwi's fifth, and final, confirmed kill.

During the remainder of April no fewer than 23 Luftwaffe aircraft, including a He 177, Ju 88Gs and 188s, Ju 52s, a He 111 and two Ju 290s, were shot down by NF XIIIs and XXXs of Nos 219, 410, 264, 488, 409, and 406 Sqns. The last aircraft downed fell on 2/3 May when Flg Off Brian Williams and Wt Off Hardy of No 605 Sqn destroyed an Fw 190 over Lecke, in Denmark.

Wg Cdr Howard Douglas Cleveland, a native of Vancouver, joined the RCAF in October 1940. 'Howie' assumed command of No 418 Sqn at the outset of 1944, and with Flt Sgt Frank Day DFM, scored four and one shared destroyed in the air and five and one shared destroyed and one damaged on the ground. His final scores came during an intruder mission over the Baltic on 16 May 1944 in FB VI MM421 *Lil' Abner*, when Cleveland destroyed a Do 217 on the ground and then forced an He 111 to crash into Kiel Bay without firing a shot. MM421 was hit in the engine by return fire, however, and the wing commander was injured and Day killed in the resulting crashlanding in Sweden. Cleveland was repatriated to Britain in June, where he received his DFC. In August 'Howie' returned to Canada, reporting in January 1945 to the Ninth Air Force on attachment, before taking command of No 418 Sqn once again in May 1945. He returned to Canada in September 1945 (*Stephen M Fochuk*)

No 100 GROUP

Bomber Command's No 100 Group was formed on 23 November 1943 after it became was obvious to all that the RAF needed a specialised bomber support force. Placed under the command of Air Commodore (later AVM) E B Addison, the Norfolk-based group was given two task to perform – its heavy bomber squadrons would be used on radio counter-measures (RCM) and 'spoofing' operations, while its Mosquito units flew loose escort duties for the main force, as well as Night Intruder operations. Some eight nightfighter squadrons were eventually equipped solely with Mosquitoes, while No 192 Sqn operated a mix of Mosquito B IVs, Halifax and Wellington X aircraft in the ELINT (Electronic Intelligence) role, monitoring German radio and radar. Throughout 1944 and into early 1945, No 192 Sqn crews listened in on enemy radio frequencies and jammed VHF transmissions. They even afforded the RAF the occasional control of German fighters through GCI.

First to join No 100 Group was No 141 Sqn which, in June 1943, had traded its Beaufighter IFs for VIFs fitted with Gee, AI Mk IV and Serrate equipment. The latter enabled the crew to 'home in' on the radar transmissions of German nightfighters, and was used in conjunction with AI Mk IV radar. In September Serrate was installed in No 141 Sqn's first Mosquito NF II, and the unit joined No 100 Group at West Raynham on 4 December. Many of the NF IIs supplied to the group were war-weary veterans of Fighter Command, and their engines often proved unreliable, as did their radar equipment. On 10 December the unit was joined by No 239 Sqn, who also received NF IIs, and then Nos 169 and 515 Sqns, who transferred to No 100 Group at Little Snoring. The group's first operation was flown on the night of 16/17 December 1943 when two Beaufighters and two NF IIs of No 141 Sqn supported the main force raiding Berlin.

The first victories occurred on the night of 28/29 January 1944 when

The NF IIs used by No 100 Group units in December 1943 had previously seen much use with Fighter Command, and serious reliability problems were experienced both with their Merlin 21s and AI radar. This photograph shows NF IIs of No 157 Sqn at Swannington in May 1944, with Leavesden-built HJ911 parked nearest to the camera. As the first in a batch of 34 NF IIs delivered to the RAF between September and November 1942, this aircraft had served with No 157 Sqn for almost two years by the time this shot was taken, and it went on to serve with Nos 141 and 307 Sqns and No 1692 Flt before being struck off charge on 19 February 1945. Its sole nocturnal success came on 27/28 June 1944 when No 141 Sqn's Sqn Ldr G J Rice and Flg Off J G Rogerson destroyed a Ju 88 over Cambrai

Flg Offs Harry White DFC and Mike Allen DFC downed a Bf 109 near Berlin and Flg Offs N Munro and A R Hurley of No 239 Sqn got a Bf 110 again near the German capital. On 30/31 January Flt Lt G J Rice and Flg Off J G Rogerson of No 141 Sqn destroyed a Bf 110 and Sqn Ldr Joe Cooper and Flt Lt Ralph Connolly an identical fighter in the Brandenburg area. In February 1944 three more enemy nightfighters were destroyed by Nos 141, 169 and 239 Sqns.

No 515 Sqn's Beaufighters were replaced by NF IIs commencing 29 February, these weary nightfighters also being used as trainers for the type – the unit began operations proper in March partially equipped with new FB VIs and flying on detachment with No 605 Sqn at Bradwell Bay. Things started well when an He 177 was destroyed by an NF II flown by No 515 Sqn's OC, Wg Cdr Freddie Lambert (with Flt Lt E Morgan), during the unit's first sortie on 5 March.

In April 1944, the Special Duty Radar Development Unit was formed at Foulsham for trials and development work on radar and various apparatus carried by No 100 Group aircraft, and on 1 May it became the BSDU (Bomber Support Development Unit). Apart from B IV and B XVI Mosquitoes, the unit also operated Beaufighters, Stirlings and Halifaxes. April had also seen No 515 Sqn move from Bradwell Bay to Little Snoring, and flew its first operation from there on the 7th.

April-May 1944 also saw Nos 85 and 157 Sqns, equipped with NF XIIs/XVIIs and XIXs, respectively, and fitted with the first AI Mk X radar sets, leave Fighter Command to join No 100 Group at Swannington. These units, and No 23 Sqn, which would also join 100 Group in June after arriving back in the UK from the Mediterranean, where they had been blasting Rommel's supply lines, were experts in the Intruder role – No 23 Sqn's FB VIs would operate from Little Snoring alongside Nos 515 and 169 Sqns, with No 1692 Flight moving to Great Massingham.

During May No 100 Group Mosquitoes claimed 18 aircraft destroyed, the first of these falling on 10/11 May when Bf 110 Wk-Nr 740179 3C+F1 of 1./NJG4 (piloted by Oberleutnant Heinrich Schulenberg) was intercepted and shot down near Ellezelles, in Belgium, by Flg Off Viv Bridges DFC and Flt Sgt Donald G 'Spider' Webb DFM of No 239 Sqn at 0010 hours. Radio Operator Oberfeldwebel Hermann Meyer recalled;

'We were shot down with one engine on fire. We could save ourselves by baling out, and came down near Flobeg. I was wounded on the skull and was badly concussed. I spent three weeks in hospital at Brussels and then had four weeks leave at home.'

Three German nightfighters fell to No 141 Sqn the following night when six Serrate Mosquitoes were despatched to Bourg Hasselt Louvain, in Belgium. Flt Lts Harry White DFC and Mike Allen DFC registered their tenth victory when they shot down a Ju 88, while a second Junkers

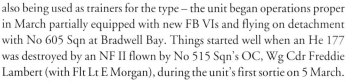

As one of No 100 Group's most successful pilots, Harry White had joined the RAF as a 17-year old in 1940, having lied about his age. On 4 August 1941 he crewed up with 18-year-old Mike Seamer Allen at No 54 OTU at Church Fenton. The following month the two of them were posted to No 29 Sqn at West Malling, where they started defensive night patrols in Beaufighters. White was eventually commissioned as a pilot officer on 26 March 1942 and, after scoring three kills and two damaged in July/August 1943, both he and Allen were awarded DFCs – Bars followed in April and October 1944. White and Allen's first Mosquito victory came on 27/28 January 1944 when they destroyed a Bf 109 near Berlin. On 15/16 February they claimed a He 177 *Beleuchter* (Illuminator), which was being used in conjunction with single-engined fighters conducting *Wilde* and *Zahme Sau* tactics against RAF bombers. The pair continued to score until their lengthy tour with No 141 Sqn came to an end in July 1944, by which time their tally had risen to 12 destroyed and three damaged. Their final claim was for a Ju 88 damaged whilst flying an NF XXX with the BSDU in January 1945 (*Mike Allen*)

55014

Oberleutnant Hans 'Fritz' Krause, a *Staffelkapitän* in 1./NJGr. 10 (he later rose to the rank of *Gruppenkommandeur* of III./NJG 11) fiddles with the strap on his flying helmet beside his Fw 190A-9/R11 (Wk-Nr 550143). Note the rod aerials for the FuG 217 *Neptun J1* radar protruding vertically out of the spine of the aircraft behind Krause, further aerials being fitted above and below the wings and forward of the cockpit – this system helped the *'Wilde Sau'* pilot indicate to flak batteries on the ground that he was 'friendly'. *'Wild Sau' geschwader* were used mainly to hunt high flying Mosquitoes at night, and although they achieved only limited success against their chosen foe, pilots like Hans Krause took a toll of the far more vulnerable, and abundant, four-engined bombers. On 20/21 April 1944 Krause was credited with shooting down a Mosquito from No 239 Sqn, flown by Sqn Ldr E W Kinchin and Flt Lt D Sellars, over Berlin. Surviving the war with a tally of 28 night victories, Krause was also a late recipient of the Knight's Cross, which he was awarded on 7 February 1945 (*via Hans Peter Debrowski*)

nightfighter from 6./NJG 2 (flown by Wilhelm Simonsohn) fell to the guns of the remarkable 46-year-old bespectacled Belgian pilot, Flt Lt Lucien J G LeBoutte, whose radar operator was Flg Off Ron Mallett – Simonsohn and his crew all baled out safely. In June Lucien LeBoutte was taken off operations and given a staff position in London, having completed two tours of operations.

On 12/13 May Viv Bridges and 'Spider' Webb enjoyed more success when they shot down Ju 88C-6 Wk-Nr 750922 D5+? of 5./NJG 3, crewed by pilot Unteroffizier Josef Polzer, radar operator Obergefreiter Hans Kluender and air gunner Gefreiter Hans Becker at Hoogcruts, near Maastricht. Only Becker survived the engagement

New crews were regularly arriving at No 100 Group stations to fly Mosquito intruder operations throughout this period. One of these comprised Wt Off Les Turner and Flt Sgt Frank Francis, who had been posted to No 169 Sqn after crewing up at No 51 OTU. Frank recalls;

'Although we had little in common on the ground, he was an excellent radar screen "reader", and our successes were in no small part due to his expertise. Until going on to ops in the Mosquito, I thought the best fighter was the Beaufighter. Seated centrally between those two great radial engines gave you a sense of power which had to be experienced to be believed. No 169 Sqn was then equipped with rather ageing NF IIs with forward and rearward looking AI Mk IV radar and armed with four 20 mm Hispano-Suiza cannon. Serviceability was a continuing problem until at the end of June 1944 we got FB VIs.

'As well as radar we also had Serrate. This was a homing device which was supposed to lock on to German nightfighter radar transmissions. It could not give range or altitude, merely direction, and while it worked after a fashion in practice (we did a two-week course on it on Beaufighters before going to the squadron), my log-book records only one instance where we got Serrate indications, and these proved abortive. However, after about a fortnight's practice both day and night, we set out on our "Freshman" op on 19 May 1944. We had in fact been scheduled for 15 May, but it was thought that the penetration was too deep for an inexperienced crew – the crew that replaced us, Plt Offs W H "Andy" Miller and Freddie Bone, had a field day that night, claiming two Ju 88s and a Bf 110 to set an unbroken squadron record.'

On 22/23 May another NJG 3 machine was downed by a Mosquito when Bf 110G-4 Wk-Nr 720050 D5+? of 3./NJG 3 was destroyed by No 169 Sqn's OC, Wg Cdr N B R Bromley OBE, and Flt Lt Philip V Truscott. Pilot Feldwebel Franz Müllebner, radar operator Unteroffizier Alfons Josten and air gunner Gefreiter Karl Rademacher were all wounded in the action but baled out successfully. Their aircraft crashed at Hoogeveen, near Groningen.

Sqn Ldr Harold 'Micky' Martin DSO, DFC (right) of 'Dambusters' fame is seen with Wg Cdr Freddie Lambert, OC No 515 Sqn, at Little Snoring in the spring of 1944. Martin was supposed to be 'resting' with the Mosquito squadron following his tour with bomber Command, but instead flew many ops and even destroyed an unidentified enemy aircraft on 26 April 1944 and an Me 410 over Knocke, in Belgium on 25/26 July – both with Flg Off J W Smith as his navigator (*Tom Cushing Collection*)

On 24/25 May three more Bf 110s were downed by No 239 Sqn crews, Raby and Flint and Hughes and Perks each destroying a Bf 110G-4 from 7./NJG 6 – Wk-Nr 730106 2Z+AR crashed at 0230 hours in a forest between Zweifall and Mulartshuette, south-east of Aachen, pilot Oberleutnant Helmut Schulte and air gunner Unteroffizier Hans Fischer both baling out, although radar operator Unteroffizier Georg Sandvoss was killed. The second Bf 110, flown by Unteroffizier Oskar Voekel, crashed five minutes later at the Wesertalsperre near Eupen, south of Aachen. Voelkel, radar operator Unteroffizier Karl Hautzenberger and air gunner Unteroffizier Günther Boehme all baled out safely. Finally, Bf 110 Wk-Nr 140032 G9+CR of 7./NJG 1 was shot down by Sqn Ldr Reeves and Plt Off O'Leary at 0115 hours, the fighter crashing at Spannum in Friesland province, in Holland. Pilot Unteroffizier Joachim Tank escaped with slight wounds, although his radar operator, Unteroffizier Günther Schröder, and air gunner, Unteroffizier Heinz Elwers, were both killed.

That same night a No 239 Sqn Mosquito crashed in Belgium, whilst a No 515 Sqn FB VI crewed by Flg Offs David Kay Foster and radar operator Robert Stanley Ling that had been sent to patrol over Leeuwarden also failed to return – they had been shot down by airfield defence flak, crashing into a hangar on the base. Both are buried in Leeuwarden Northern General Cemetery.

On 5/6 June Nos 85 and 157 Sqns flew their first operations with No 100 Group when 21 Serrate Mosquitoes were despatched to northern France. The former unit put up 12 aircraft over the Normandy invasion beaches, whilst four Mosquitoes from No 157 Sqn (and ten from of No 515 Sqn) made intruder raids on Belgian and Dutch airfields. Two victories were claimed by 100 Group, both of which were scored by No 239 Sqn crews. The first kill fell to Flg Offs W R Breithaupt DFC and J A Kennedy DFC, who downed Ju 88G-1 Wk-Nr 710454 of 5./NJG 3 20 kilometres north of Spiekeroog, killing the pilot, Unteroffizier Willi

No 239 Sqn's Flg Off Viv Bridges DFC and Flt Sgt Don 'Spider' Webb DFM who, on 10/11 May 1944, destroyed Bf 110 Wk-Nr 740179 3C+F1 of 1./NJG 4, piloted by Oberleutnant Heinrich Schulenberg near Ellezelles, in Belgium. They repeated this success two nights later when they downed Ju 88C-6 Wk-Nr 750922 of 5./NJG 3, flown by Unteroffizier Josef Polzer, at Hoogcruts, near Maastricht. On 31 May/1 June Bridges and Webb scored their third kill (a Bf 110), followed on 7/8 July by yet another Bf 110, near Charleroi, for their fourth, and last, victory of the war (*Don Webb Collection*)

No 515 Sqn's Plt Off David Foster was shot down and killed by airfield flak defences around Leeuwarden on 27/28 May 1944, his stricken Mosquito crashing into a hangar on the base
(*Theo Boiten via Tom Cushing*)

Hammerschmitt, radar operator, Unteroffizier Friedrich Becker and air gunner, Feldwebel Johannes Kuhrt, in the process. The second victory was claimed by Flt Lt Dennis Welfare DFC* and Flg Off D B 'Taffy' Bellis DFC*, and took the form of Bf 110 Wk-Nr 440272 G9+NS of 8./NJG 1, which crashed at 0054 on the northern beach of Schiermonnikoog – pilot Unteroffizier Adolf Stürmer, radar operator Unteroffizier Ludwig Serwein and gunner Gefreiter Otto Morath were all killed.

On 8/9 June Do 217K-3 Wk-Nr 4742 6N+OR of Stab III./KG 100 was shot down by Wg Cdr Bromley and his radar operator, Flt Lt Truscott, in the Paris area. Pilot Oberleutnant Oskar Schmidtke, observer Unteroffizier Karl Schneider, wireless operator Unteroffizier Helmuth Klinski and flight engineer Unteroffizier Werner Konzett all died in the crash. June 1944 proved to be a fruitful month for No 100 Group Mosquitoes, with some 33 kills being claimed.

On 11 June No 85 Sqn OC, Wg Cdr Michael Miller DFC, downed a Bf 110 at Melun, and two nights later Flt Lt James G Benson of No 157 Sqn destroyed a Ju 188 at Compiégne. On 13/14 June Les Turner and Freddie Francis scored their first kill when they claimed a Ju 88, the former firing at the bomber from 300-400 yards and setting its port engine alight. Burning fiercely, the Ju 88 turned to port, forcing Turner to take evasive action by turning in the same direction until the Mosquito was on its back. He regained control as the Ju 88 hit the ground and exploded.

On 15/16 June Bf 110 Wk-Nr 5664 G9+IZ of 12./NJG 1 was destroyed by Sqn Ldr F S Gonsalves and Flt Lt B Duckett of No 85 Sqn near Tongres, between St Trond and Maastricht. Wounded pilot, Unteroffizier Heinz Bärwolf, and radar operator Unteroffizier Fischer baled out, but gunner Obergefreiter Edmund Kirsch was killed. The following night Ju 88 Wk-Nr 710590 of 1./NJG 2 crashed in the Pas de Cancale, having probably fallen victim to Flg Offs Andy Miller DFC and Freddie Bone of No 169 Sqn. All three crewmen were killed.

On 17/18 June a Bf 110 of NJG 1 was downed at 0230 by Flg Off P S Kendall DFC* and Flt Lt C R Hill, the aircraft crashing on Soesterberg airfield – all three crewmen were killed. That same night also saw Flt Lt G F Poulton and Flg Off John Neville of No 239 Sqn come across Ju 88s orbiting a beacon. The pilot fired at two of them, as Neville recalls;

'We claimed one destroyed after it plunged earthwards thoroughly on fire, and the second likewise plunged down with one engine on fire which fairly soon went out. This we claimed as damaged, and both were credited to us (the first was Ju 88G-1 Wk-Nr 710866 of 8./NJG 2 – it crashed on Volkel airfield, killing two of the crew and wounding the third).'

Flg Off Robert Ling was Flg Off Foster's navigator on that fateful patrol on the night of 27/28 May 1944. Both he and his pilot are buried in Leeuwarden Northern General Cemetery
(*Theo Boiten via Mrs Beryl Boucher-Ling*)

On 21 June 1944 Bf 110G Wk-Nr 440076 G9+NS of 8./NJG 1 was destroyed at 1519 by Sqn Ldr

Paul Rabone DFC and Flg Off F C H Johns, the fighter crashing on Eelde airfield, killing all three crewmen. Four days later Nos 85 and 157 Sqns flew to West Malling for anti-Diver patrols.

On the night of 27/28 June No 239 Sqn crews shot down an Me 410 east of Paris and an Fw 190 and a Ju 88 near Brussels, while No 141 Sqn claimed two Ju 88s (one near Cambrai and the other south of Tilburg) and a No 515 Sqn crew destroyed a Ju 88 over Eindhoven.

One of the Ju 88s lost that night was G-1 Wk-Nr 710455 of 4./NJG 3, which crashed at Arendonk, in Belgium, killing its three-man crew killed, whilst the Ju 88 claimed by No 239 Sqn was credited to Flt Lt Donald R 'Podge' Howard and Flg Off Frank A W 'Sticky' Clay. They had closed to within 50 ft of their target to make certain that it was indeed a Ju 88, before dropping back and blasting it apart with two bursts of cannon fire. Their Mosquito was hit by flying debris in the explosion, forcing Howard to nurse the aircraft back to Manston on a single engine.

On 30 June/1 July Flt Lt D J Raby DFC and Flt Sgt S J Flint DFM, also from No 239 Sqn, destroyed Ju 88 Wk-Nr 711114 of 5./NJG 2 over France. They had stalked the Junkers nightfighter for quite some time, being fired at by the Ju 88's gunner, although his tracer passed harmlessly over the top of the Mosquito. Raby eventually fired a two-second burst from 450 ft and saw strikes all along the port-side fuselage and wing which eventually resulted in the port engine bursting into flames. He pumped another two-second burst into the doomed Ju 88, which exploded, scattering debris into the path of the charging Mosquito. As it fell vertically to earth, Raby continued to pepper the machine, finally breaking away just before another explosion tore the wings off the night-fighter. It crashed south-east of Dieppe with a massive explosion.

Intruder Mosquitoes, meanwhile, continued their Night Ranger operations over the continent and were rewarded with a mounting tally of victories. Some 26 aircraft were claimed destroyed by No 100 Group units in July 1944, the first of these falling to Flg Offs P G Bailey and J O Murphy of No 169 Sqn on the 5th/6th when they claimed Ju 88 Wk-Nr 751065 R4+? of 5./NJG 2 near Chartres. Pilot Oberfeldwebel Fritz Far-

This NF XIX wears the SD codes of No 157 Sqn, and is seen parked in the unit's dispersal near St Peter's Church, in Haveringland, on whose land part of RAF Swannington airfield was sited. No 157 Sqn was equipped with NF XIXs from May 1944 through to April 1945

rherr and gunner Obergefreiter Heinz Boehme were killed, but radar operator Gefreiter Josef Schmid succeeded in baling out with wounds. That same night FB VIs of No 23 Sqn flew their first Intruder operations with a series of sorties against enemy airfields.

Two nights later Sqn Ldr G J Rice and Flg Off Jimmy Rogerson of No 141 Sqn almost certainly downed Bf 110G-4 Wk-Nr 730006 D5+? of 2./NJG 3 west of Chievres, in Belgium. Two of the three-man crew succeeded in baling out safely, although the third was killed. That same night, Bf 110G-4 Wk-Nr 110028 C9+HK of 2./NJG 5

crashed near Compiégne, killing pilot Leutnant Joachim Hanss and air gunner Feldwebel Kurt Stein, although radar operator Unteroffizier Wolfgang Wehrhan escaped with wounds. It is believed that this Bf 110 was one of the two aircraft downed by Sqn Ldr J S Booth DFC* and Flg

Flg Off Henri Cabolet and Flt Lt R V Smith of No 239 Sqn are interrogated at West Raynham following the completion of a sortie by Section Officer Jean Barclay (*Tom Cushing Collection*)

On 17/18 June 1944 No 239 Sqn's Flt Lt Geoffrey E Poulton and Flg Off Arthur J Neville destroyed a Ju 88 and damaged another near Eindhoven. They are seen here in this staged photograph later in 1944, by which time Poulton had become a squadron leader, and 'A' Flight Commander, and Neville had been promoted to flight lieutenant – both men had also received the DFC by this point in their tours too

Off K Dear DFC of No 239 Sqn.

A week later, on 14/15 July, No 189 Sqn's Les Turner and Freddie Francis caught a Bf 109 near Auderbelck during a Serrate patrol. Turner blasted the enemy fighter from 150 ft, whereupon it flipped onto its back and emitted a bright flash as it hit the ground. They landed back at Great Massingham with slight damage from fragments of the enemy aircraft. On 20/21 July Bf 110G-4 Wk-Nr 730218 G9+EZ of 12./NJG 1 fell victim to No 169 Sqn's previously successful

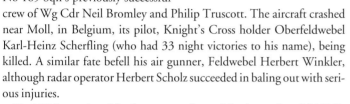

On 27/28 June 1944 No 141 Sqn's Sqn Ldr Graham J Rice (left) and Flg Off Jimmie G Rogerson (above) used NF II HJ911 (see photo on page 64) to destroy a Ju 88 over Cambrai, followed on 7/8 July by Bf 110G-4 Wk-Nr 730006 D5+ of 2./NJG 3 west of Chievres, Belgium, in NF II DZ298 (*Richard Doleman*)

crew of Wg Cdr Neil Bromley and Philip Truscott. The aircraft crashed near Moll, in Belgium, its pilot, Knight's Cross holder Oberfeldwebel Karl-Heinz Scherfling (who had 33 night victories to his name), being killed. A similar fate befell his air gunner, Feldwebel Herbert Winkler, although radar operator Herbert Scholz succeeded in baling out with serious injuries.

No 169 Sqn enjoyed further success three nights later when Bf 110G-4 Wk-Nr 730036 G9+ER of 7./NJG 1 was downed by Flt Lt R J Dix and Flg Off A J Salmon at low level near midnight. The aircraft crashed near Balk in the Friesland Province of Holland, its pilot, Feldwebel Heinrich Karl Lahmann and air gunner Unteroffizier Günther Bouda, both baling out. However, radar operator Unteroffizier Willi Huxsohl was killed.

Things got no better for NJG 1 as the night went on, for at 0125 hours a second 7.*Staffel* Bf 110G-4 (Wk-Nr 730117 G9+GR) was shot down north of Deelen airfield, although all three crewmen escaped without injury – Flg Offs N Veale and R D Comyn of No 239 Sqn claimed at Bf 110 this night. Just over 20 minutes later a third NJG 1 Bf 110 was lost when III.*Gruppe* machine (or possibly another 7.*Staffel* aircraft) Wk-Nr 441083 G9+OR was downed at 0147 hours whilst coming in to land at Leeuwarden. The nightfighter crashed at Rijperkerk, north of the base, killing pilot, Hauptmann Seigfried Jandrey, and radar operator, Unteroffizier Johann Stahl, although air gunner Unteroffizier Anton Herger escaped with injuries. This aircraft was possibly downed by a 2nd TAF Mosquito from No 141 Sqn crewed by Plt Offs Doug Gregory and D H Stephens, who returned to West Raynham claiming a Ju 88 destroyed.

On 28/29 July Ju 88G-1 Wk-Nr 713649 R4+KT of 9./NJG 2, flown by Hauptmann August Speckmann, with Oberfeldwebel Wilhelm Berg as flight engineer, air gunner Unteroffizier Otto Brueggenkamp and Oberfeldwebel Arthur Boos as radar operator, was shot down over France – only Boos survived. This aircraft was probably one of the two Ju 88s destroyed by No 141 Sqn's Doug Gregory and D H Stephens and Harry White and Mike Allen. Gregory let fly at his target with a one-and-a-half second burst which set the Ju 88 alight. They watched it go down burning into solid cloud at 8000 ft, and after a few seconds the undercast lit up as the Junkers nightfighter exploded upon hitting the ground near Metz.

Late in July Nos 515 and 23 Sqns at Little Snoring began flying day-

light escort sorties for heavy bombers attacking Bordeaux. They continued daylight operations into August by switching to Day Rangers, which saw them engaging air and ground targets within a wide, but specified, area – the most successful No 100 Group Day Ranger was performed on 29 October 1944 when two No 515 Sqn crews, comprising Flt Lt E L'Amie and Flg Off R A Smith and Plt Off Terry A Groves DFC and Flt Sgt R B 'Doc' Dockeray DFM, downed nine and damaged five aircraft. Further daylight sorties were flown in September by FB VIs of No 23 Sqn when the unit escorted No 100 Group Fortress IIIs on 'Big Ben' patrols.

On 20 August Nos 85 and 157 Sqns had completed their anti-Diver duties and resumed Bomber Support sorties from Swannington, although by this stage victories achieved by No 100 Group Mosquitoes were on the wane largely due to successful German counter-measures to the Serrate homing device. Indeed, during this month only eight aircraft were destroyed – one of them fell to No 169 Sqn's Les Turner and Freddie Francis on 26/27 August, their victim being Ju 88G-1 Wk-Nr 710542 D5+BR of 7./NJG 3, flown by Leutnant Achim Woeste.

During the engagement, Turner allowed the target to pull away to a separation distance of 1000 ft before opening fire. His aim was good, however, and the Ju 88's port engine burst into flames, forcing the bomber into a series of gentle diving turns to starboard, trailing a spiralling plume of grey smoke in its wake. The Mosquito crew followed, firing intermittently and observing strikes all over the fuselage. Woeste and Unteroffizier Anton Albrecht were fatally hit during one of these attacks, leaving Unteroffizier Heinz Trippe and Gefreiter Karl Walkenberger (who were both wounded) to bale out. Soon after Turner and Francis saw a 'tremendous flash' as the Ju 88 crashed near Mulsum, east of Bremen.

Between 6/7 and 12/13 September, eight more German nightfighters fell to No 100 Group Mosquitoes, and on the 13th/14th Flt Lt Bill House and Flt Sgt Dennis McKinnon of No 85 Sqn were sent on a patrol over Germany to look for a ninth victim to add to the tally. This unit had been particularly short of navigators when McKinnon had been hurriedly posted in straight from training, and he had therefore never been to Night Flying Training School. In fact, he had never been in an aircraft that had had to fire its guns before! MacKinnon recalls;

'I guided Bill onto an Me 110 near Koblenz, and managed to get

On 30 September No 515 Sqn's Sqn Ldr Henry Morley and Flt Sgt Reg Fidler were returning from a Day Ranger to the Munich-Linz-Vienna area in FB VI PZ440 when their aircraft was hit by a Swiss 20 mm flak battery whilst flying between Konstanz and Zurich at a height of just 200 ft. With its port engine knocked out, the Mosquito was quickly intercepted by four Swiss Morane MS.406 fighters and escorted to Dübendorf airfield, over which PZ440's starboard engine also quit, forcing Morley to crash-land near Volketswil. Both men suffered only minor injuries (*via Tom Cushing*)

A newly-delivered NF XXX of No 85 Sqn taxies out at Swannington at the start of a Night Intruder over Germany. The unit started swapping its NF XVII for definitive NF XXXs in September 1944

No 157 Sqn's OC, Wg Cdr K H P Beauchamp DSO, DFC, is seen with his navigator, Flt Lt L Scholefield DFC, at Swannington in late 1944. On 12/13 December 1944 this pair had damaged a Bf 110 south-east of the Ruhr during a chase which had taken them over Aschaffenburg airfield during a patrol in support of Bomber Command attacks on Essen. Scholefield had initially got a contact at six miles range which Beauchamp chased, before dropping back to 600 ft astern and firing two short bursts. Strikes were seen on the starboard wing, followed by a large showers of sparks, but visual contact was then lost. As was so often the case, the AI radar had also been upset by the firing of the guns, resulting in the target being lost. Beauchamp and Scholefield had better luck just over a week later, however, when they destroyed a Ju 88 west of Koblenz on 21/22 December
(*Mrs Edna Scholefield Collection*)

behind it without the crew being aware of us. Bill opened fire and I thought it was us who were being attacked. The noise, to me, was terrifying, but to the enemy it must have been terrible. The whole plane just blew up in front of our eyes.'

Their victim was Bf 110G-4 Wk-Nr 440384 G9+EN of 5./NJG 1. Its pilot, Oberleutnant Gottfried Hanneck, who had six kills of four-engined bombers to his credit, baled out, although radar operator Unteroffizier Erich Sacher and gunner Unteroffizier Willi Wurschitz were killed when the aircraft crashed at Birresborn at 2335 hours – Hanneck experienced being shot down by a British nightfighter once more on 1 February 1945.

On 17/18 September 11./NJG 1 lost Bf 110G-4 Wk-Nr 740358 G9+MY when it was downed east of Arnhem by one of the RAF's most successful nightfighter crews, Flg Offs 'Ginger' Owen DFM and Viv McAllister DFM again from No 85 Sqn. Unteroffiziers Walter Sjuts, Herbert Schmidt and Ernst Fischer were all killed. The same pair also downed Bf 110G-4 Wk-Nr 740757 G9+GZ of 12./NJG 1 minutes later – Unteroffiziers Heinz Gesse, Josef Kaschub and Obergefreiter Josef Limberg died in the action.

				1944	SQDN
ME. 110.	W/COM. MILLER. D.F.C. 2 BARS -	F/o. SYMON.	11™ JUNE	85
ME. 110.	F/LT PHILLIPS.	F/LT SMITH	12™	85
JU. 188.	F/LT BENSON. D.F.C.	F/LT BRANDON	12™	157
JU. 88.	F/LT TWEEDALE.	F/o CUNNINGHAM.	14™	157
JU. 188.	F/LT BURBRIDGE. D.F.C.	F/LT SKELTON.	14™	85
JU. 88.	F/LT THOMAS.	P/o. HAMILTON	14™	85
ME. 110.	S/L. GONSALVES.	F/LT DUCKETT	15™	85
JU. 188.	F/LT MATTHEWS.	W/O. PENROSE.	15™	157
ME. 110.	F/o. KENDALL. D.F.C. & BAR	F/LT HILL.	16™	85
JU. 88.	F/LT BURBRIDGE. D.F.C.	F/LT SKELTON	23™	85
JU. 88.	F/LT MATTHEWS.	W/o. PENROSE.	12™ JULY	85
ME. 110.	LT SANDIFORD.	LT THOMPSON	14™	157
JU. 188.	S/L BURBRIDGE. D.F.C.	F/LT SKELTON. D.F.C. 11™ SEPT		85
JU. 188.	S/L BENSON. D.F.C. - BAR	F/LT BRANDON. D.F.C. 11™		157
JU. 188.	S/L BENSON. D.F.C. - BAR	F/LT BRANDON. D.F.C. 11™		157
ME. 109.	F/LT KENDALL. D.F.C. BAR	F/LT HILL. D.F.C.	12™	85
ME. 110.	F/LT DOLEMAN.	F/LT BUNCH. D.F.C.	12™	157
ME. 110.	F/LT HOUSE.	F/SGT McKINNON	13™	85
ME. 110.	F/o. OWEN.	F/o. McALLISTER. D.F.M 17™		85
ME. 110.	F/o. OWEN.	F/o. McALLISTER. D.F.M 17™		85
ME. 410.	F/LT VINCENT.	F/o. MONEY.	29™	157
JU. 188.	F/LT PHILLIPS.	F/LT SMITH.	28™	85
ME. 110	F/LT MATTHEWS.	W/O. PENROSE.	7™ OCT	157
JU. 88.	S/L. BURBRIDGE. D.F.C.	F/LT SKELTON. D.F.C 14™		85
ME. 110.	F/L. NOWELL.	W/O. RANDALL	15™	85
JU. 188.	S/L. BURBRIDGE. D.F.C.	F/LT SKELTON. D.F.C 19™		85
JU. 88.	S/L. DOLEMAN.	F/LT BUNCH. D.F.C.	19™	157

Swannington's 'Hun' Score Board reveals just how productive Nos 85 and 157 Sqns were between 11 June and 19 October 1944

By the end of September No 100 Group Mosquitoes had claimed 14 aircraft destroyed, and in October another 17 were claimed. On 6/7 October Ju 88G-1 Wk-Nr 710639 D5+EV of 10./NJG 3 was downed by Flt Lt Gallacher and Plt Off McLean of No 141 Sqn, the aircraft crashing near Groningen. Pilot, Oberleutnant Walter Briegleb, flight engineer, Unteroffizier Brandt, and gunner Unteroffizier Braeunlich, were all wounded, whilst radar operator Feldwebel Paul Kowalewski was killed.

On 7/8 October Flt Lt Jimmy Mathews and Wt Off Alan 'Penny' Penrose of No 157 Sqn picked up a contact at six miles west of Neumünster while on a high-level support sortie. Mathews narrowed the range, and as they got a visual at 1000 yards, the target straightened out. It was recognised as a Me 410 with long-range tanks, and Mathews opened fire with a short burst from 100 yards dead astern. Strikes were seen and a small explosion occurred in the starboard engine, before a second burst set the power-plant alight. The aircraft dived into the ground and exploded.

Paul Mellows and Dickie Drew of No 169 Sqn were also on patrol that night, and they sought targets over Egmond, as the former recalls;

'We arrived in the patrol area at 2005, flying at 15,000 ft. Two beacons flashing were seen near two airfields, so we decided to investigate. At 2022 hours an AI contact was obtained hard port at maximum range, our height being 14,000 ft. We closed to 7000 ft when the target commenced hard turns to port through a number of orbits. Then he straightened out and climbed at low speed, and we closed to 100 ft to identify the aircraft as a Ju 88. I dropped back and opened fire at 500 ft. I observed strikes between the starboard engine and fuselage before the Ju 88 peeled off to port and visual was lost, but Dickie held the contact at 10,000 ft range.

'I closed in again, losing height to 14,000 ft and obtained another visual while in a hard starboard turn at 500 ft on an enemy aircraft which was losing height and turning to starboard. However, visual could not be held and no further AI contact was obtained on the enemy aircraft, which was inside maximum range. We continued to patrol the area, where three aerodromes were now lit, until 2120 hours at heights ranging between 7000 and 15,000 ft but no further contacts were obtained. We set course for base and claimed a Ju 88 damaged.'

Flt Sgt R B 'Doc' Dockeray DFM and Plt Off Terry A Groves DFC of No 515 Sqn destroyed a Bf 110 in the air, and damaged several Bf 109s on the ground, during a legendary Day Ranger with Flt Lt F T L'Amie and Flg Off J W Smith on 29 October 1944 that saw nine aircraft shot down and five damaged (*Tom Cushing Collection*)

On 4/5 November 1944 No 85 Sqn's Sqn Ldr Branse Burbridge DSO* DFC* and Flt Lt Bill Skelton DSO* DFC* shot down three Ju 88s and this Bf 110 from II./NJG 1 north of Hangelar airfield. The Messerschmitt crashed into the Rhine at 2150 hours, killing pilot Oberleutnant Ernst Ranze, although radar operator Obergefreiter Karl-Heinz Bendfeld and the gunner baled out safely. Burbridge and Skelton finished the war as the top scoring nightfighter team in the RAF, with 21 aircraft destroyed, two probables, one damaged and three V1s also destroyed

German losses this month included Ju88G-1 Wk-Nr 712312 2Z+EB of I./NJG 6 on 19/20 October which was possibly downed by Flt Lt G D Bates and Flg Off D W Field of No 141 Sqn. It crashed at Vaihingen/Marksdorf north-east of Pforzheim, in Germany, killing pilot Oberleutnant Wilhelm Engel and radar operator Unteroffizier Ernst Dressel. This same night, Sqn Ldr 'Dolly' Doleman and Flt Lt 'Bunny' Bunch were possibly downed Ju 88G-1 Wk-Nr 714510 2Z+CM of 4./NJG 6, which crashed at Murrhardt, near Heilbron, also in Germany. Pilot Unteroffizier Georg Haberer and radar operator Unteroffizier Ernst Dressel were both killed.

On 22/23 October No 169 Sqn's Les Turner and Freddie Francis flew their 32nd trip – a Serrate patrol to Denmark. They chased a contact west of Nissun Fjord at 15,000 ft for five minutes before finally, at 2000 yards range, they obtained a visual on a Ju 88. It was standing on its port wing and tight turning, but as it peeled off Francis held him on Serrate, and following a hectic three-minute dogfight, range was once again closed to 2000 ft. Turner throttled back and put down full flap, before opening fire with his cannons at about 400 yards. The Ju 88 peeled off to starboard and Turner fired again, but it was ineffective.

By now the Mosquito was flying at just 145 mph with full flap, the fighter being buffeted about by the slipstream from the Ju 88. The crew followed the German down to 4000 ft, where they lost radar contact in the ground returns. Turner and Francis patrolled off the coast for another 30 minutes with 'no joy', returning to base with only a 'damaged' claim. However, the former is convinced that the Ju 88 crashed, as he spotted a fire on the ground some ten minutes after their attack. Soon after this action, Turner was promoted to flying officer and Francis to warrant officer, being awarded the DFC and DFM respectively.

On 4/5 November two more Bf 110s almost certainly fell to No 100 Group Mosquito crews, a II./NJG 1 machine being shot down at 1900 at a height of 20,000 ft. Pilot Unteroffizier Gustav Sario was wounded and baled out, but radar operator Unteroffizier Hienrich Conrads and gunner Obergefreiter Roman Talarowski were both killed. The second Bf 110, also from II./NJG 1, was one of four kills claimed that night by No 85 Sqn ace crew, Sqn Ldr Branse Burbridge DSO*, DFC* and Flt Lt F S Skelton DSO*, DFC*. The Bf 110 crashed into the Rhine near Hangelar airfield at 2150, taking with it pilot Oberleutnant Ernst Runze, although radar operator Obergefreiter Karl Heinz Bendfield managed to bale out.

Two other Bf 110s were also shot down that night, G-4 Wk-Nr 440648 G9+RS of 8./NJG 1 possibly being destroyed by a Mosquito nightfighter. It crashed at Bersenbrück, north of Osnabrück, and although pilot Feldwebel Willi Ruge baled out wounded, radar operator Unteroffizier Helmut Kreibohm and gunner Obergefreiter Anton Weiss were both killed. A Mosquito also claimed the life of 15-victory night ace Leutnant Heinz Rolland of IV./NJG 1 who, along with radar operator Feldwebel Heinz Krüger and gunner Unteroffizier Karl Berger, died when their Bf 110 crashed near Wezel, in Germany.

On 6/7 November two Ju 88G-6 aircraft were lost, Wk-Nr 620396 R4+KR of Stab IV./NJG 3 being downed by a Mosquito over Marienberg. Pilot Hauptmann Ernst Schneider was killed, but both radar operator Oberfeldwebel Mittwoch and gunner Unteroffizier Kaase baled out safely. Wk-Nr 620583 R4+TS of 11./NJG 3 was destroyed in combat near Paderborn, although its crew escaped with their lives.

'A' Flight of No 157 Sqn pose together at a misty Swannington during the winter 1944-45. Flight Commander Sqn Ldr James Benson, is seated in the centre of the front row, with Brian Blundell, Hannawin and Sib Davidson to his left. Bill Tofts is seated immediately behind Davidson
(*Brian Whitlock Blundell Collection*)

As the sun sets a Mosquito nightfighter awaits the arrival of its crew at Swannington in late 1944 (*Brian Whitlock Blundell Collection*)

As a result of the large-scale use of the Mosquito in late 1944, German nightfighter defences were forced to change their tactics, and this seriously reduced their efficiency. For example, one *geschwader* of roughly 100 three-man crews lost 24 crews killed, ten missing and 15 wounded in just three months. It was at around this time that the real 'Moskitopanik' started, and from then on all routine losses suffered on operations due to mechanical failure or pilot error were also attributed to the Mosquito!

The fighter's increased reputation heightened the German nightfighter crews' despondency, and their demoralisation was complete late in 1944 when they had to resort to throwing out 'Düppel' ('Window') as a routine in order to mislead and distract Mosquito nightfighters. Top scoring German nightfighter pilot Hauptmann Heinz-Wolfgang Schnaufer (121 victories) attributed his continued survival to the fact that he did not only weave, but actually carried out what he described as 'steep turns' from take-off to landing in order throw off any Mosquito attempting to track him down. He even continued to weave when in AI contact with a bomber. Schnaufer's impression was that none of the top German nightfighter pilots dared to climb to the height of the attacking bombers until the last moment, remaining very low, or at '*Ritterkreuz* Height', for they knew that if they flew higher, they would never survive to receive the decoration. Schnaufer recalled that the only time he felt free from fighters was whilst actually in the bomber stream, but he also added that because of the threat of Mosquito intruders 'it was impossible to relax even then'.

Hauptmann Hans Krause, with 28 destroyed, quoted an instance in the Ruhr when he was intercepted over the target area and pursued for 45 minutes, enduring frequent 'visuals' on the Mosquito as it came into range throughout this time. He took violent evasive action in azimuth and height and by going through cloud, but this failed to shake off the fighter. He finally succeeded in evading only by flying to a district in the Ardennes that he knew really well and flying, as he said, 'Down a valley below the level of the hills'. This confirmed in his mind the exceptional standard of the British AI radar. German nightfighter crews now had to fly at tree-top height to their locator beacons, which caused many accidents with aircraft flying into the ground. An alternative technique for returning to base was also adopted when the situation allowed it, the pilot landing after flying a straight approach from 10,000 ft. Krause used this technique whenever possible for 'it had the added advantage of giving you plenty of time to bale out if you were shot down by a Mosquito'.

MOSQUITO MENACE

'Moskitopanik' reached a peak during December 1944 when no fewer than 36 enemy nightfighters were shot down. On 2/3 December Capt Weisteen of No 85 Sqn had started the scoring by claiming Bf 110G-4 Wk-Nr 180382 of 12./NJG 4, which had taken off from Bonninhardt at 2047. It crashed at 2145 near Lippborg, with only the pilot, Leutnant Heinz-Joachim Sclage, surviving the action. Flt Lt W Taylor and Flg Off J N Edwards of No 157 Sqn also shot down a nightfighter that same evening – possibly Ju 88 Wk-Nr 714819 3C+WL of 3./NJG 4 – which crashed at Rheine. Pilot Oberfahnrich Erhard Pfisterhammer, radar operator Unteroffizier Wolfgang Sode and the air gunner were all wounded. Two nights later Mosquitoes performed a 'spoof' raid on Dortmund while the Main Force attacked Heilbronn and Karlsruhe. German nightfighters were sent to intercept the former force and waited in the area for about 15 minutes for the attack to start. All they found were high intruders, however, and their losses were heavy.

On this night No 100 Group units shot down five, and probably destroyed a sixth, with Flt Lts R T 'Dickie' Goucher and C H 'Tiny' Bulloch of No 85 Sqn destroying two of the nightfighters. Squadronmates Flg Offs 'Ginger' Owen and J S V McAllister earned the distinction of scoring the unit's 100th victory (and their 12th) when they downed Ju 88G-1 Wk-Nr 714152 of 6./NJG 4, which crashed near Krefeld. Pilot Unteroffizier Wilhelm Schlutter was wounded, whilst radar operator Unteroffizier Friedrich Heerwagen and gunner Gefreiter Friedrich Herbeck were both killed.

On 6/7 December Flt Lt J O Mathews DFC and Wt Off A Penrose

NF XIX TA446/RS-Q of No 157 Sqn was written off in an emergency belly landing carried out by its crew, Flt Lt A Mackinnon and Flg Off Waddell, at the USAAF's 44th Bomb Group base at Shipdham, in Norfolk, on 16/17 January 1945. This incident was caused by an in-flight engine failure triggered by the flying debris from an exploding Ju 188 shot down by the crew near Fritzler (*via Steve Adams*)

No 239 Sqn's Flt Lts S L 'Dickie' Drew DFC and A B A Smith are seen at interrogation at West Raynham after complete a Night Intruder sortie. The former was navigator for Flt Lt Paul Mellows DFC of No 169 Squadron on the night of 1/2 February 1945 when they shot down a Bf 110 (*Tom Cushing Collection*)

DFC destroyed a Bf 110 and a Ju 88 (Wk-Nr 712268 of I./NJG 4, which crashed near Giessen killing the air gunner, Gefreiter Alfred Gräfer). Flt Lt Edward R Hedgecoe DFC and Flt Sgt J R Whitham, who were attached to the Fighter Interception Unit (FIU), also destroyed a Bf 110 west of Munster that same night – possibly G-4 Wk-Nr 740078 G9+HZ of 12./NJG 1, which crashed north-west of Handorf). This aircraft was being flown by *Staffelkapitän* Hauptmann Hans-Heinz Augenstein, who was killed, along with his radar operator Günther Steins. One of the *Nachtjagd*'s leading aces, Augenstein had scored 46 night victories (including 45 RAF night bombers) and been awarded the Knight's Cross on 9 June 1944. Although wounded during the fight, bordschütze Unteroffizier Kurt Schmidt managed to bale out.

On the night of 12/13 December five more German nightfighters were downed by No 100 Group Mosquitoes, with No 85 Sqn's Hedgecoe and Whitham (although then still attached to the FIU), destroyed two more Bf 110s to take the former's score to eight or nine destroyed. The unit's Sqn Ldr Branse Burbridge and Flt Lt F S also added a Ju88 and a Bf 110 to their rising score, the Ju 88G-1 (Wk-Nr 714530 of 6./NJG 4) crashing at Gütersloh airfield. All three crewmen (pilot Unteroffizier Heinrich Brune, radar operator Unteroffizier Emil Hoffharth and air gunner Unteroffizier Wolfgang Rautert) were killed.

Three more Bf 110s fell on the night of 17/18 December, whilst Flt Lt William Taylor and Flg Off J N Edwards destroyed He 219A-O Wk-Nr 190229 G9+GH of 1./NJG 1 24 hours later, the 'Uhu' (Owl) crashing at Suedlohn and killing radar operator Unteroffizier Günther Heinze, although pilot Unteroffizier Scheürlein baled out safely. Flg Off Edwards was killed four days later during a landing accident which also involved Flt Lt Taylor back at Swannington. On the night of 22/23 December No 85 Sqn's ace pairings of Burbridge and Skelton and Owen and McAllister again enjoyed success, with the former downing a Bf 110 and the latter a hat trick of victories comprising two Ju 88s and a Bf 110. Ju 88G-6 Wk-Nr 621441 2Z+HK of II./NJG 6 crashed at Landstuhl, killing pilot Oberfeldwebel Max Hausser, radar operator Oberfeldwebel Fritz Steube and gunner Feldwebel Ernst Beisswenger, whilst Ju 88G-6 Wk-Nr 621436 2Z+DC, also from II./NJG6, crashed at Lebach. Unteroffizier Werner Karau survived, but the remaining two crewmen were killed.

On Christmas Eve No 100 Group supported two raids, one by 104 Lancasters of No 3 Group on Hangelar airfield, near Bonn, and the other by 97 Lancasters and five Mosquitoes of Nos 1 and 8 Groups on the marshalling yards at Cologne/Nippes. At Cologne good Oboe marking resulted in extremely accurate bombing, with losses restricted to just five Lancasters downed during the raid and two more crashing in England.

Some 18 German aircraft were shot down, including five by four Mosquito crews from No 100 Group – Flt Lt Mathews and Wt Off Penrose of No 157 Sqn got a Ju 88G near Cologne for their seventh kill of the campaign, whilst squadronmates 'Dolly' Doleman and 'Bunny' Bunch went two better with three Bf 110s in the Cologne/Duisburg area (taking their score to nine), including Bf 110G-4 Wk-Nr 740162 G9+OT of 9./NJG1 flown by Hauptmann Heinz Strüning, a 56-night victory ace, and winner of the Knight's Cross with Oak leaves. He was shot down at 2200 and crashed at Bergisch Gladbach/ Rheinland, and although his bordfunker and Bordschütze baled out safely, Strüning was killed when he hit the tail of his Bf 110. His body was found some two months later.

In a night for aces, No 157 Sqn's Sqn Ldr James Benson DFC and Flt Lt Lewis Brandon DSO, DFC also destroyed a Bf 110 to raise their score to nine, while ranking Norwegian ace of World War 2, Capt Svein

This graphic photograph shows the damage suffered by Flt Lts Paul Mellows and 'Dickie' Drew's NF XXX NT252 as a result of their combat with a Bf 110 near Stuttgart on 1/2 February 1945
(*Paul Mellows Collection*)

NF XXX RS-S of No 157 Sqn is seen sitting in the snow at Swannington during the bitter winter of 1944-45
(*Brian Whitlock Blundell Collection*)

No 192 Sqn's Flt Lt 'Hank' Cooper
DSO, DFC, navigator-radar operator,
and Flg Off Kelt, RNZAF, pilot, pose
in front of B IV 'H' at Foulsham, in
Norfolk, during the winter of 1944-
45. This dedicated ELINT (electronic
intelligence) squadron within No
100 Group also operated Halifaxes
and, for radar and radio
investigation, Mosquito NF II DZ292.
All their aircraft were fitted with
various receivers for the detection of
German nightfighter AI frequencies
over the continent, which they
recorded on Bagful and Blonde
recording equipment
(*'Hank' Cooper Collection*)

Heglund DFC (he had scored 11 kills flying Spitfires with No 331 Sqn in 1942-43 – see *Osprey Aircraft of the Aces 5 - Late Mark Spitfire Aces* for further details), with Flg Off Robert O Symon, downed his second of three Bf 110 kills achieved with No 85 Sqn, 20 miles north of Frankfurt.

The last of the 36 aircraft to fall to No 100 Group in December comprised two Ju 88s and a He 219 claimed on on New Years Eve. The latter, He 219A-2 Wk-Nr 290194 G9+KL of 3./NJG 1, was shot down by Flt Lts Paul Mellows and S L 'Dickie' Drew of No 169 Sqn in an NF XXX whilst attached to No 85 Sqn at Swannington during interception trials with the new Mk X AI radar. Mellows recalls;

'We had obtained a contact at six miles range and chased slowly to port and climbing from 15,000 ft to 18,000 ft. While the contact was still well above, another came in at three miles range from the west nearly head on. This was found to be at our height, so we turned to starboard as it passed us and came in 4000 ft behind. A visual was obtained at 2000 ft on four white exhausts, and on closing to 400 ft, twin tail fins were seen, and shortly after, black crosses on the blue undersurfaces of the wings were seen in the light of a searchlight. On the strength of this I fired a two-second burst from slightly below, causing debris to fly off and starting a small fire in the fuselage. Another two-second burst caused an explosion, by the light of which Dickie clearly saw the dihedral and slanting fins of a He 219, which I confirmed. A further short burst set him alight, and from 1000 ft to starboard we saw him climb for a few seconds before plunging to earth, where he exploded with a bright orange flash at 1824 hours. Throughout the combat the He 219 was flying straight and level, and appeared to have no knowledge of our presence.'

The He 219 crashed at Schleiden, south-west of Cologne, although its crew safely baled out despite being wounded.

81

A further 16 aircraft were claimed shot down by No 100 Group Mosquitoes in January 1945, Dickie Goucher and 'Tiny' Bullock of No 85 Sqn getting the month off to a flying start with two aircraft destroyed on 1/2 January. They claimed a Ju 188 ten miles north of Münster, while Ju 88G-6 Wk-Nr 621364 2Z+CP of 5./NJG 6 crashed at Dortmund, killing its four-man crew. These successes were Goucher and Bullock's last of the war, taking their tally to five aircraft and two V1s destroyed.

Another top scoring team in Flt Lts 'Ben' Benson and 'Brandy' Brandon of No 157 Sqn notched up their ninth, and last, combined victory (Benson had a tenth to his credit from his Defiant days with No 141 Sqn in 1940) on 5/6 January when they downed He 219A-O Wk-Nr 190188 G9+CK of 2./NJG 1 south of Wesendorf – pilot Oberfeldwebel Josef Stroelein was killed but radar operator Unteroffizier Kenne baled out safely. That same night No 515 Sqn's Flt Lt A S Briggs and Flg Off Rothwell almost certainly downed Ju 88 Wk-Nr 620513 R4+CD of III./NJG 2, which crashed onto Jagel airfield killing its crew.

Flt Lt K D Vaughan and R D Mackinnon shot down two of those aircraft that fell during January, including possibly Ju88G-1 Wk-Nr

FB VI PZ459 was assigned to 'A' Flight of No 515 Sqn at Little Snoring, where it was coded 3P-D 'D-Dog' and flown almost exclusively by Plt Off Leslie George 'Dutch' Holland (pictured) and Flt Sgt Robert 'Bob' Young. Note the AI Mk XV ASH (Air-Surface H) nose radome – ASH was designed as a wing-mounted radar, but it was found to be unsuitable for fitment to the Mosquito's slender wing, so it was installed in a 'thimble' radome in the nose instead. Following service with No 515 Sqn, PZ459 was briefly used by No 141 Sqn before being placed in storage. It was eventually sold as scrap in July 1947 (*Leslie Holland via Tom Cushing*)

NF XXX NT585 of No 125 Sqn makes a fast pass down the starboard side of the Mosquito camera aircraft over typically flat Norfolk countryside in the early autumn of 1944. This particular nightfighter had seen service with the Polish-manned No 307 Sqn prior to its arrival at No 125 Sqn's Coltishall base in October 1944. Its final frontline posting was with No 151 Sqn, with whom it remained until the unit disbanded in 1946. The veteran NF XXX (or more accurately NF 30, as it was redesignated postwar) was finally sold as scrap in July 1948 (*Richard Doleman*)

FB VI RS566 of No 515 Sqn is seen parked at dispersal at Little Snoring in late 1944. Issued to the unit almost straight from the Hatfield factory, this aircraft later served briefly with No 141 Sqn until it transitioned to NF XXXs in April 1945. Following a brief spell in storage, RS566 was one of around 57 FB VIs sold to the *Armée de l'Air* – it was delivered to its new owners in August 1947 (*Tom Cushing Collection*)

710818 D5+EP of Stab./NJG 3, which crashed south-east of Freidberg on the 14th/15th, killing its crew.

On the night of 28/29 January 1945 Paul Mellows and Dickie Drew tried to score another victory using the new Mk X AI radar whilst temporarily at Swannington. Departing their base at 2050, they undertook a high level support patrol to Stüttgart for some 'beacon bashing', as Mellows recalls;

'Shortly after completing the patrol in "Beacon Fritz", a single white flare was seen to the north-west, presumably over Darmstadt. We proceeded in that direction, and Biblis airfield was seen to be lit and had a canopy of four searchlights two miles to the west. From 6000 ft, three single-engined aircraft could be seen outlined against the snow on the airfield. As there were no signs of airborne activity, and time was short, I decided to make an attack. I approached the airfield from the south-west and attacked one of the single-engined aircraft, believed to be a Fw 190, with two three-second bursts from a height of 1500 ft to 1000 ft. I observed no results from the first burst, but strikes were seen on, and around, the fuselage from the second burst. Defences opened up when we were over the centre of the airfield, but without results.'

In February ten German aircraft were destroyed by Mosquitoes of No 100 Group, plus a probable on on the first night of the month. The 1st/2nd also marked the return of Oberleutnant Gottfried Hanneck of 5./NJG 1 to action, having been wounded whilst being shot down by House and MacKinnon on 13/14 September 1944. Flying Bf 110G-4 Wk-Nr 730262 G9+CN with a new crewmen radio operator Feldwebel Pean and gunner Unteroffizier Glöckner, Hanneck and was promptly shot down once more by a Mosquito! It is believed that his adversary was either a No 157 or 239 Sqn Mosquito, for Sqn Ldr Ryall and Plt Off Mulroy of the former unit claimed a Bf 110 'probable' over Oberolm, while OC No 239 Sqn (and future five-kill ace), Wg Cdr Walter Gibb DSO, DFC, and Flg Off R C Kendall DFC, also destroyed a Bf 110 over Mannheim in NF XXX NT309.

Also on 1/2 February, Flt Lt Paul Mellows and Dickie Drew of No 169

Sqn almost certainly downed Bf 110G Wk-Nr 730370 2Z+EL of 3./NJG 6, which crashed south of Stüttgart – its three-man crew were all killed.

No 239 Sqn crews were prominent on the night of 7/8 February, with Bf 110G-4 Wk-Nr 730322 G9+HR of 7./NJG 1 being destroyed west of Soest by Flt Lt D A D Cather DFM and Flt Sgt L J S Spicer BEM. Pilot Feldwebel Heinz Amsberg and radar operator Unteroffizier Matthias Dengs were both killed, while gunner Gefreiter Karl Kopperberg baled out wounded.

Squadronmates Flt Lts A J Holderness and Walter Rowley DFC's victim was also a Bf 110, the former quickly closing up to just 200 ft below and behind the contact, identifying it, and dropping back to about 250 yards, before opening fire with his 20 mm cannon. Debris immediately flew off the enemy fighter and its port engine caught fire. Then the nose went up and the Bf 110 commenced a steep climb, which Holderness tried to follow, still firing. Although he throttled right back the Mosquito was rapidly overtaking the nightfighter, and Holderness had to pull away quickly to starboard. Just then the Bf 110 seemed to stall and flick over to port, the left engine now a mass of flame. Rowley could still see burning pieces coming off the Messerschmitt when it went into the cloud. Almost simultaneously there was a terrific white flash which lit up the clouds. Holderness followed through the undercast to come out at 4000 ft on the altimeter, and there was the Bf 110, burning immediately below them.

On 13/14 February 'Podge' Howard and 'Sticky' Clay at BSDU had a very eventful night which ended with them attaining ace status. While

No 239 Sqn personnel gather outside their crew room at West Raynham for an informal group photograph. They are, from left to right, at the rear, squadron OC, Wg Cdr W F Gibb DSO, DFC (who, on 5/6 March 1945, with Flg Off R C Kendall DFC, destroyed two Ju 88s at Nürnburg to add to their Bf 110 and Fw 190 claims during February), unknown, Dicky Da Costa, Wt Off Tanner (obscured, and wearing dark glasses), Flt Sgt Briggs, Flt Lt Wimbush and Wt Off 'Chalky' White. Front row, left to right, unknown, Sqn Ldr A J Holderness (who, with Flt Lt W Rowley, destroyed a Bf 110 on the night of 7/8 February), Peter Poirette and an unknown Australian (*Graham 'Chalky' White*)

No 141 Sqn's Flt Sgt Frank H Baker, navigator-radar operator, and his pilot, Flg Off (2Lt) R D S 'Hank' Gregor, USAAF. On 14/15 March 1945 'Hank the Yank and Frank' were on a lone ASH patrol in the Frankfurt-Mannheim area in support of the bombers attacking Zweibrucken, near Saarbrucken, when they shot down a UEA coming into land at Lachen airfield. The enemy aircraft exploded under their nose just as they began pulling out after closing rapidly to 100 ft. The explosion illuminated the area, and almost at once they drew light flak and were coned by a searchlight, which Gregor dodged by turning into it and diving. This victory was No 141 Sqn's final air-to-air kill of the war (*Molly Baker Collection*)

Wg Cdr W K Davison, OC No 85 Sqn from January 1945, is surrounded by his flight crews at Swannington in May 1945 (*via Mick Jennings*)

serving with No 239 Sqn at West Raynham, they had destroyed three aircraft between June and October 1944. As an experienced crew, their input into the development of the AI Mk X and Serrate IV systems (the latter with a lowered frequency band of 80 m/cs), proved to be of great value. On this night (in NF XIX MM684) Clay obtained a contact at about five miles, 30° to port and down. A 'visual' was obtained at 1000 ft, and at 600 ft the aircraft was identified as a Bf 110. Howard fired a short burst, but no strikes were seen. He increased deflection and fired another burst, and this time there were hit registered all over the starboard engine, wing root and the starboard side of the cockpit. A fire erupted in the starboard wing root, and the Bf 110 turned over to port ablaze and dived down into cloud. Seconds later there was a vivid white explosion as the nightfighter hit the ground.

Barely two minutes had passed when another contact appeared crossing from starboard to port above them at a range of 12,000 ft. Howard and Clay turned after it, and at 600 ft separation the aircraft was identified as a Bf 110. Howard opened fire, missed, and the Bf 110 promptly rolled into a starboard bank. The NF XIX pilot then fired a one-second burst which struck the cockpit, fuselage and port wing root. The Bf 110

From left to right, Wg Cdr Buchan DSO, DFC*, Sqn Ldr 'Dolly' Doleman DFC, Sqn Ldr 'Jimmy' Mathews DFC* and Flt Lt 'Bunny' Bunch DFC* are seen on VE-Day, 8 May 1945. After a barren run early in 1944, Doleman teamed up with Bunch, and on their first sortie together on 12/13 September they destroyed a Bf 110. Doleman and Bunch finished the war with ten victories, two shared destroyed, one probable one and one shared damaged and three V1s destroyed. Mathews' tally stood at nine kills by war's end, all scored flying with 'Penny' Penrose as part of No 157 Sqn. The pair damaged a further six aircraft, as well as destroying five V1s (*Richard Doleman Collection*)

then dived away to starboard and Howard gave him another burst, which set his port engine alight and caused debris to fly off. He then dived vertically into cloud, 'burning very well'. One of the downed aircraft was Bf 110G Wk-Nr 480164 C9+? of 5./NJG 5, which crashed near Bodenbach, in the Frankfurt area, killing the crew.

Thirteen aircraft were downed by No 100 Group Mosquitoes during March, the first two of which were both Ju 88s destroyed on the night of 5/6 March, and both to Wg Cdr Gibb and Flg Off Kendall DFC in NF XXX NT361. Ju 88G-6 Wk-Nr 622319 C9+GA of Stab./NJG 5 crashed near Chemnitz, killing both the pilot, NJG 5's Kommodore, and Knight's Cross holder, Oberstleutnant Walter Borchers (who was also a 59-victory ace, 16 of which had been scored by day and the remaining 43 by night), and his radar operator, Leutnant Friedrich Reul.

The second Junkers 'twin' to fall to Gibb was Ju 88G-6 Wk-Nr 622318 C9+NL of 3./NJG 5, which also crashed near Chemnitz. Pilot Unteroffizier Hans Dorminger and his crew were all killed. Two weeks later on 18/19 March, Gibb and Kendall downed an He 219 in NF XXX NT271 at Witten to take their score to five. Pilot Hauptmann Baake, *Gruppenkommandeur* of I./NJG 1, and his radar operator, Unteroffizier Bettaque, baled out safely. A third He 219 was brought down as one of the last victories of the month when, on 20/21 March, Flt Lt G C Chapman and Flt Sgt J Stockley of No 85 Sqn destroyed a Bf 110 and a He 219V-14. The latter, Wk-Nr 190014 of 3./NJG 1, was being flown by Oberleutnant Heinz Oloff, *Staffelkapitän* of 3./NJG 1, at the time.

By 17/18 April (the last month of the war in which No 100 Group victories were recorded) 11 aircraft had been shot down by day and night Mosquito intruders. On 4/5 April ex-No 169 and 85 Sqn veteran Sqn Ldr Tim Woodman (with Flt Lt Neville) destroyed a Bf 109 west of Magdeburg whilst serving with the BSDU – this kill took Woodman's final wartime tally to seven destroyed and one damaged. On 9/10 April No 151 Sqn's OC, Wg Cdr Howard Kelsey DFC*, and Flt Lt L E M Smith DFC DFM destroyed a Ju 188 south-east of Hamburg for their fifth victory while with No 100 Group (and Kelsey's eighth overall, plus three aircraft destroyed on the ground).

On 19/20 April 'Podge' Howard and 'Sticky' Clay claimed a Ju 88 destroyed near Fyn Island, off southern Denmark, after picking up a contact crossing from starboard to port above them at a range of four miles.

They turned behind the contact at a distance of 5000 ft when a 'visual' was obtained on the aircraft. Howard later wrote;

'With the aid of glasses, the aircraft was identified at 1500 ft as a Ju 88. A short burst from dead astern at 250 yards caused the outer half of the port wing to fall away. The aircraft rolled on its back, hit the ground, spread over a wide area and caused a number of small fires. We landed back at base at 0104 and submitted a claim for one Ju 88 destroyed.'

April was not without its losses, however. On the 17th a No 239 Sqn Mosquito crashed at Melsbroek, in Belgium, and on 18/19 April a No 141 Sqn Mosquito, crewed by Kiwis Wt Off Ronald G Dawson and Flg Off Charles P D Childs, failed to return from an attack on the NJG 6 airfield at Neubiberg. They had been downed by Leutnant Wolfhard Galinski, a 20-year-old pilot from 8./NJG 6, but he had not been flying his Bf 110 at the time. After landing from a night ground attack mission, Galinski, and the rest of his unit, came under attack by two Mosquitoes and he and Leutnant Koegler (the unit's communications officer) had manned AA guns and shot down one of the attackers – the aircraft crewed by Dawson and Childs. They were buried at Durnbach War cemetery.

No 515 Sqn had flown its first Master Bomber sortie on 13/14 April, dropping Target Indicators followed up by the bombs and incendiaries of the Mosquito force. No 100 Group Mosquitoes had, meanwhile, performed 'spoofing' raids on airfields and cities. The following night five FB VIs of No 141 Sqn, fitted with 100-gal Napalmgel drop tanks – carried out the first of 13 'Firebash' raids on airfields at Neuruppin and Juterbog, near Potsdam and Berlin. On 24/25 April Nos 456 and 151 Sqns flew their last operation when four NF XXXs from the former unit and six from the latter undertook Night Rangers, while No 141 Sqn again carried out a Napalm attack, this time on Munich-Neubiberg airfield. The final victory awarded to No 100 Group went to No 515 Sqn's Wg Cdr Howard Kelsey and Flt Lt L E M Smith in FB VI RS575 on 24/25 April.

In May No 100 Group completed its wartime work with a series of Napalm ('Firebash') raids on north German targets, the final operation being flown on 2/3 May. A record number of 106 No 100 Group aircraft took part in raids on Flensburg and Hohn airfields in Schleswig Holstein, Westerland and Jagel. Simultaneously, 126 Mosquitoes from No 8 Group of the Pathfinder Force followed in the wake of 16 of its aircraft, and 37 from No 100 Group, in attacks on Kiel. Honn and Flensburg airfields were bombed with Napalm and incendiaries directed by Master Bomber, Sqn Ldr Griffiths of No 515 Sqn, whilst No 169 Sqn's NF XIXs raided Schleswig and Westerland and others dropped Napalm on Jagel.

Les Turner, who was making his ninth, and last, trip of his second tour with No 169 Sqn, was amongst those who attacked Jagel. He recalls;

'By now I had had enough of destruction and, while I could see the surrounding buildings, I decided to drop my 200 gallons of Napalm on the airfield. The war was obviously not going to last much longer. The opposition was quite intense, and as I followed Keith Miller (later to become famous as an Australian test cricketer), the light Flak aimed at him was passing worryingly close to us. Keith said that one of his drop tanks hung up and slewed him to starboard – but for this, he reckoned that he would have got caught in the flak. As it was, we still regrettably lost one of our crews – such a waste so near to the end.'

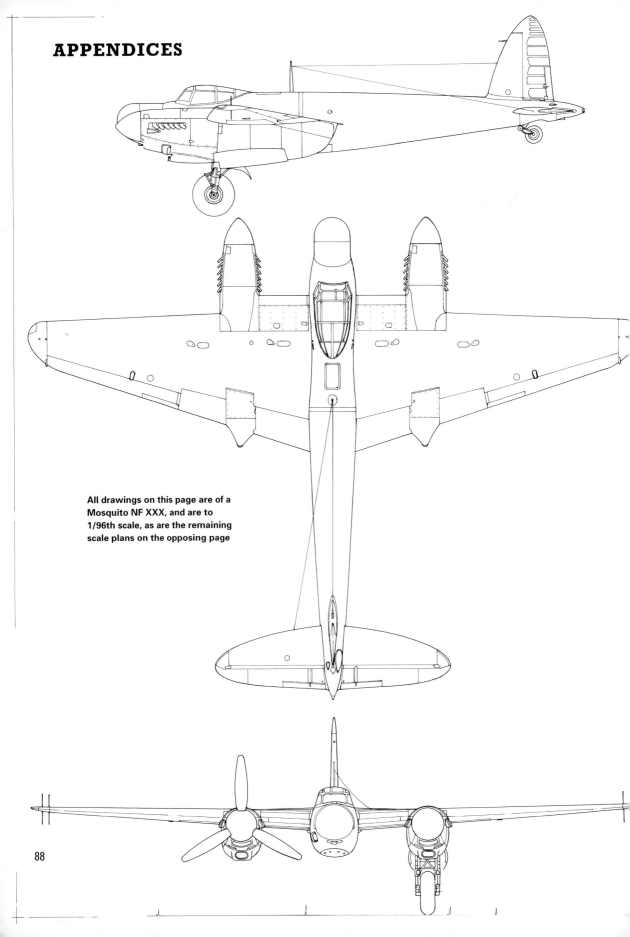

APPENDICES

All drawings on this page are of a
Mosquito NF XXX, and are to
1/96th scale, as are the remaining
scale plans on the opposing page

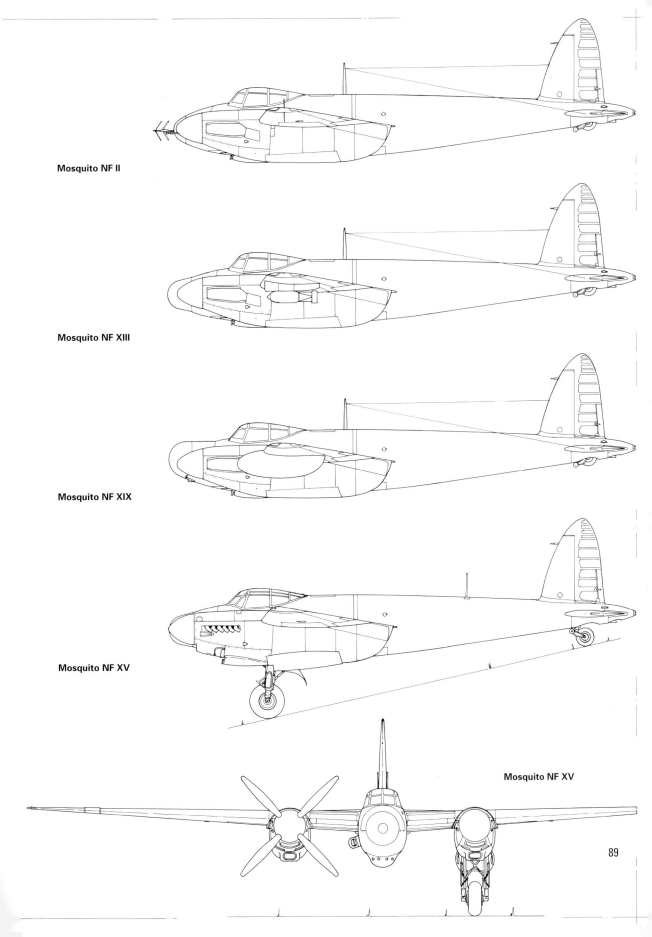

Mosquito NF II

Mosquito NF XIII

Mosquito NF XIX

Mosquito NF XV

Mosquito NF XV

89

APPENDICES

FIGHTER COMMAND MOSQUITO SQUADRONS

No 23 Sqn	To No 100 Group in May 1944 and to Fighter Command 1945
No 25 Sqn	
No 29 Sqn	Air Defence of Great Britain (ADGB) to No 148 Wing, No 85 (Base) Group, 2nd TAF, on 1/5/44. To No 147 Wing in June 1944. Back to ADGB in 26/8/44
No 68 Sqn	
No 85 Sqn	To No 100 Group on 1 May 1944, then to Fighter Command in 1945
No 96 Sqn	
No 108 Sqn	Mediterranean
No 125 Sqn	
No 141 Sqn	To No 100 Group in November 1943
No 151 Sqn	
No 157 Sqn	To No 100 Group on 1 May 1944
No 169 Sqn	To No 100 Group on 7 December 1943
No 219 Sqn	No 147 Wing, No 85 (Base) Group, from 28/8/44 to 7/5/45
No 239 Sqn	To No 100 Group in December 1943
No 255 Sqn	Italy
No 256 Sqn	Mediterranean
No 264 Sqn	ADGB to No 141 Wing, No 85 (Base) Group, 2nd TAF, on 19/12/43 (administered as such from 10/3/44). Left No 141 Wing 19/6/44. To No 148 Wing on 26/6/44. To UK on rest, 23/9/44. To No 148 Wing from 8/1/45 to 7/5/45
No 307 Sqn	
No 406 Sqn	
No 409 Sqn	To No 148 Wing, No 85 (Base) Group, 2nd TAF, on 30/3/44
No 410 Sqn	To No 141 Wing, No 85 Group, 2nd TAF, on 12/5/44. To No 147 Wing, No 85 Group, from 18/6/44 to 7/5/45
No 418 Sqn	To No 136 Wing, 2nd TAF, from 21/11/44 to 7/5/45
No 456 Sqn	Nos 10/11 Groups, Fighter Command
No 488 Sqn	To No 147 Wing, No 85 (Base) Group, 2nd TAF, on 12/5/44. Disbanded 26/4/45
No 515 Sqn	To No 100 Group on 15/12/43
No 600 Sqn	Italy
No 604 Sqn	To No 141 Wing, 2nd TAF, from 26/4/44 to 2/5/44, to No 147 Wing, No 85 (Base) Group, 2nd TAF, until 23/9/44. To UK for rest. To No 148 Wing, No 85 Group, 31/12/44. Non-operational from 15/4/45 (disbanded 18/4/45)
No 605 Sqn	To No 136 Wing, No 2 Group, 2nd TAF, from 21/11/44 to 7/5/45

COLOUR PLATES

1

Mosquito fighter prototype W4052, A&AEE Boscombe Down, July 1941

Fighter prototype W4052 differed from the prototype Mosquito bomber in having two 1460-hp Merlin 21s fitted, as well as a flat bullet-proof windscreen and a solid nose, housing an AI radar antenna and four machine guns. Constructed at Salisbury Hall, it was flown out of a field adjacent to the assembly hangar on 15 May 1941 by Geoffrey de Havilland Jnr. W4052 had completed its handling trials at Boscombe Down by the end of July 1941, and after experiencing a belly-landing at Hogsnorton airfield (now Panshanger) on 19 April 1942, W4052 was repaired and subsequently used to test various airframe and radar modifications with the FIU (Fighter Interception Unit) at Ford. Having survived the war, this historic aircraft was unceremoniously sold for scrap on 28 January 1946.

2

NF II W4087/RS-B of No 157 Sqn, Castle Camps, March 1942

This aircraft arrived at St Athan-based No 32 MU for AI radar installation on 13 February 1942, and on 9 March it became one of the first NF IIs issued to No 157 Sqn at Castle Camps. Used principally for operational training whilst with this unit, W4087 then joined No 1422 Flight at Heston on 5 May 1942. Here, the aircraft was modified to carry a Turbinlight in the nose, flying in this experimental fit for the first time on 1 December 1942. It was subsequently sent to Wittering on 7 January 1943 to carry out frontline trials with a crew from No 532 Sqn, before being passed on to No 85 Sqn at Hunsdon the following month. By this stage of the war the development of more effective airborne radar had rendered the airborne searchlight obsolete, so in August 1943 W4087 returned to No 1422 Flight, who used it until the autumn of 1944 for general radio and radar trials work. The fighter was finally Struck off Charge (SOC) on 30 January 1946.

3

NF II 'Special' DD670/YP-S of No 23 Sqn, crewed by Wg Cdr B R O'B 'Sammy' Hoare DFC* and Plt Off Cornes, Ford, July 1942

DD670 was one of twenty-five 'Special' Intruder models built for No 23 Sqn with their AI radar equipment deleted. On 6/7 July 1942 Wg Cdr B R O'B 'Sammy' Hoare DFC* and Plt Off Cornes used the aircraft to destroy a Do 217 16 miles east Chartres. Two nights later Sqn Ldr K H Salisbury-Hughes registered the fighter's second and third kills when he shot down a Do 217 over Etampes and a He 111 near Evreux. Finally, on 30/31 July 'Sammy' Hoare and Wt Off J F Potter destroyed a UEA over Orleans again in DD670. This aircraft later served with Hunsdon's Station Flight, before being passed on to secondline units like Nos 51 and 60 OTUs. Finally grounded near the end of the war, it then became instructional airframe 4780M, before being SOC on 31 January 1946.

4

NF II DD739/RX-X of No 456 Sqn, RAAF, Colerne, September 1943

Although a veteran of frontline operations with Nos 85, 157 and 456 Sqns, DD739's sole combat kill came on 3/4 July 1943 when No 157 Sqn's Flt Lts James Gillies Benson DFC and Lewis Brandon DFC used it to destroy a Do 217 over St Trond, this victory being the former's fourth of the war. Promoted to wing commander by VE-Day end, Benson (who also received a Bar for his DFC and the DSO) eventually achieved a tally of ten aircraft destroyed and four damaged, plus six V1s also destroyed – Like Benson, Brandon had also won a DFC* and DSO by May 1945. He and Brandon had originally crewed up while on Beaufighter IFs in August 1941. Following several month of action, DD739 passed to No 456 Sqn, RAAF, which had begun converting to the NF II at Valley in the spring of 1943. Coded RX-X, the aircraft was also suitably adorned with the unit's unofficial kangaroo roundel marking in the centre of the crew entry door. Moving into the frontline with the unit following its posting to Middle Wallop in March 1943, DD739 flew a series of Day and Night Intruder operations into France until lost on a Mahmoud Bomber Support patrol to Kassel, south of Hannover, on 3/4 December 1943 – its crew, Plt Offs Tommy May and Les Parnell, were both posted Missing in Action.

5

NF II HJ911/TW-A of No 141 Sqn, crewed by Sqn Ldr Graham J Rice, RAAF, and Flg Off Jimmie G Rogerson, RAAF, West Raynham, 27/28 June 1944

As late as 1943-44 many surviving NF IIs were refurbished, receiving new engines and equipment, including AI Mk IV or V radar sets, and then issued to No 100 Group. NF II HJ911 was one such aircraft, having been used extensively by Nos 157 (as RS-H) and 307 Sqns, before being reworked and sent to No 141 Sqn in early 1944, where it became TW-A. A veteran of many night patrols, HJ911 achieved two kills during the war, both of which were credited to Sqn Ldr Graham J Rice, RAAF and Flg Off Jimmie G Rogerson, RAAF. The first was a Ju 88 over Cambrai on the night of 27/28 June 1944, followed on 7/8 July by a Bf 110G-4 thought to be Wk-Nr 730006 D5+? of 2./NJG 3, which crashed west of Chievres, in Belgium. HJ911 later passed to No 1692 Flight in the autumn of 1944, before finally being SOC on 19 February 1945.

6

NF II DZ706/YP-P of No 23 Sqn, crewed by Flt Sgt Rudd and Sgt Messingham, Luqa, Malta, 10 July 1943

A well-travelled and well-used NF II, Hatfield-built DZ706 initially served with No 301 Ferry Training Unit (FTU) and No 1 Overseas Aircraft Delivery Unit (OADU) before joining Malta-based No 23 Sqn, where it was coded YP-P – the cat marking painted below the cockpit was devised by its regular pilot at the time, Flt Sgt Rudd. No 23 Sqn operated NF IIs from Luqa (with detachments to Pomigliano and Alghero) between December 1942 and August 1943, when the first FB VIs began to arrive in the Mediterranean. The unit continued to fly intruder sorties against Axis forces in Italy, North Africa and Sicily until posted back to the UK to join No 100 Group in May 1944. No 23 Sqn's first aerial victory (a Ju 88) fell to Sqn Ldr Philip Russell and Plt Off E G Pullen on 8 January 1943 during an Intruder to Tunis airfield. DZ706 was also credited with a kill when Rudd and Messingham claimed a Ju 88 probably destroyed south of Rome on 10 July and an Me 210 off the 'toe' of Italy on 18 days later. This aircraft had returned to England by the autumn of 1943, where it was passed firstly to the Royal Aircraft Establishment (RAE) and then the Telecommunications Flying Unit (TFU), before being SOC on 21 April 1945.

7

NF II DD636/PS-D of No 264 Sqn, Predannack, May 1943

NF II DD636 was delivered to the RAF on 7 May 1942 and served for just under a year with the Handling Squadron at the Empire Central Flying School at Hullavington. On 16 April 1943 Predannack-based No 264 Sqn took it on charge, coding the aircraft PS-D. Within a month (on 11 May to be exact), DD636 had been intercepted and damaged by Fw 190s during a Day Ranger over France. Once repaired, the aircraft was posted across the airfield to fellow Predannack residents No 307 'City of Lvov' Sqn on 7 August 1943, and thence to No 157 Sqn, again at the Cornish coastal base, on 9 November 1943. DD636's time with the latter unit was to last just nine days, however, for on 19 November its crew was forced to ditch in the Channel during an 'Instep' patrol after suffering an engine failure.

8

NF II/PR II DD744 of No 60 Sqn, SAAF, Castel Benito, Tripoli, August 1943

This NF II was one of a pair of fighters converted to PR II standard through the fitment of cameras and issued to No 60 Sqn, SAAF at Castel Benito, Tripoli, on 8 August 1943. DD744 flew the unit's first sortie on 15 February 1944 and was eventually SOC in November of that same year.

9

NF II W4079/RS-F of No 157 Sqn, Castle Camps, June 1942

NF II W4079 is finished in the then standard RDM2 smooth nightfighter scheme and wears No 157 Sqn's RS codes. Allocated to the unit on 12 June 1942, it attained its only aerial kill on 28/29 March 1943 when Flg Off John Roger Beckett, RAAF (on 23 March 1944 now Flt Lt Beckett of No 605 Sqn, and his navigator, Flg Off Fred D Topping, were killed in FB VI HX823/UP-K during a Ranger to Gardelegen) and Flt Sgt Phillips shared in the destruction of Do 217E4 U5+NM Wk-Nr 4375 of 4./KG 2 with a No 68 Sqn Beaufighter off Southwold. Pilot Feldwebel Paul Huth, gunner Unteroffizier Werner Hans Burschel, observer Oberleutnant Gottfried Thorley and radio operator Unteroffizier Konrad Schuller were all killed. Following its tour with No 157 Sqn, W4079 was sent back to de Havilland on 25 September 1943 for reworking, and then t to RAE on 2 January 1944. From there it passed through a

succession of secondline units, being issued to No 10 MU on 12 March 1944, No 218 MU on 22 May and finally No 51 OTU at Cranfield on 5 August. It was still with the latter unit when, on 29 November, W4079 crashed and was destroyed. Unusually, the aircraft retained its RDM2 finish throughout its RAF career.

10

NF II HJ711/VI-P of No 169 Sqn, crewed by 'B' Flight Commander Sqn Ldr Joseph Aloysius Hayes 'Joe' Cooper and Flt Lt Ralph D Connolly, Little Snoring, January 1944

Having served with No 60 OTU and then No 141 Sqn, HJ711 became the regular mount of No 169 Sqn's Sqn Ldr J A H 'Joe' Cooper (who designed the No 169 Sqn crest, dominated by a hunting horn, based on its motto, 'Hunt and Destroy') and Flt Lt Ralph D Connolly in late 1943. Prior to joining the unit, Cooper – a pre-war lance corporal cavalryman in the 4th Hussars, and an accomplished boxer – had been one of Bob Braham's flight commanders with No 141 Sqn at West Raynham in 1943, where he had crewed up with Connolly, an Income Tax inspector from Dulwich, in South London. Cooper and Connolly damaged a Ju 88 on 18 January 1943 flying a Beaufighter, but then had to wait just over a year (to 30/31 January 1944) to score their premier Mosquito kill, and No 169 Sqn's, in HJ711 when they destroyed Bf 110G-4 Wk-Nr 740081 D5+LB of Stab.III/NJG 3, which crashed at Werneuchen, east of Berlin. HJ711 was subsequently lost on the night of 15/16 March 1944 during a Bomber Support mission to Stuttgart, its pilot, Flt Lt W W Foster, RCAF being captured and navigator, Flg Off J H Grantham, killed.

11

NF II DZ726/TW-Z of No 141 Sqn, crewed by Flg Offs Harry E White DFC and Michael S Allen DFC, West Raynham, February 1944

Issued to No 410 Sqn during the winter of 1943, DZ726 was slightly damaged on the night of 15 April 1943 when squadron OC, Wg Cdr F W Hillock, and his navigator, Flt Lt P O'Neill-Dunne, flew through HT cables during a patrol over Apeldoorn, in Holland – the aircraft brought back over 300 ft of copper cable tangled around its wings and tail. Returned to de Havilland in order to allow major repairs to be effected within the Hatfield works, the aircraft was reissued to No 141 Sqn on 18 October 1943, where it was coded TW-Z. On 15/16 February 1944 Flg Offs Harry E White DFC and Michael S Allen DFC used it to down a He 177 near Berlin, which gave them their fifth kill (and thus ace status) – the crew had opened their account back on 4 August 1941 in Beaufighter VIF V8713. Altogether, White and Allen destroyed 11 aircraft with No 141 Sqn (nine of them flying NF IIs) and one with a BSDU NF XXX, as well as damaging a further four (two of these on Mosquitoes). DZ726 was eventually lost without trace during an AI exercise on 16 May 1944 whilst being flown by Flg Off J P Watkins and Flt Sgt T Pantry.

12

NF II (Modified) DZ659/ZQ-M of the Fighter Interception Unit (FIU), Wittering, 1943

Painted in standard Intruder finish, with Smooth Night

undersurfaces and spinners, this Mosquito was the original trials aircraft for both the American SCR 720 (AI Mk X) and (later) 729 Eleanora radar, fitted in the distinctive blunt Universal nose radome. The aircraft survived the war to SOC on 28 February 1946.

13
NF XV DZ385 of the High Altitude Flight, Northolt, early 1943

First flown on 3 January 1943, DZ385 was one of just five Mosquito NF XVs constructed with the express purpose of attaining altitudes in excess of 45,000+ ft as a response to the threat posed by the Ju 86 high altitude bomber. Prototype MP469 was the first Mosquito built with a pressurised cabin, and it flew for the first time on 8 August 1942. The NF XV was essentially a modified B IV, fitted with an AI Mk VIII radar in its nose and powered by two-stage 1680 hp Merlin 72/73 or 1710 hp 76/77 engines driving three- or four-bladed airscrews. In order to save weight, and thus boost its performance even more, the NF XV's armament comprised just four .303-in machine guns in a special under-belly 'blister'. MP469 was delivered to the newly-formed High Altitude Flight at Northolt on 16 September 1942, but this, and the Fighter Interception Unit at Ford (which received DZ366, DZ385, DZ409 and DZ417), never had cause to use them operationally as the Ju 86s ceased flying over Britain. All five were then passed to 'C' Flight of No 85 Sqn at Hunsdon, where they saw limited service between March and August 1943 (DZ385 was 'K-King'), before some were passed on to the RAE at Farnborough for pressure cabin research. Following its use with the FIU and No 85 Sqn, DZ385 was last flown by No 1409 Flight, after which it was grounded and issued to the School of Technical Training at Cranwell in October 1944 as instructional airframe 4884M.

14
FB VI NS997/G/VI-C of No 169 Sqn, crewed by Flt Lt R J Dix and Flg Off A J Salmon, Great Massingham, July 1944

Part of a production run of 250 FB VIs built at Hatfield between February and May 1944, NS997/G was issued new to No 169 Sqn at Little Snoring, in Norfolk, in late March 1944. By June the unit had moved to Great Massingham, and it was from here that Flt Lt R J Dix and Flg Off A J Salmon set off on a Night Intruder over Germany on 23/24 July in NS997 that resulted in them shooting down a Bf 110 near Kiel. In February 1945 No 169 Sqn re-equipped with NF XIXs, and NS997/G was flown to Marshall's of Cambridge for overhaul, before being placed in storage firstly with No 273 MU in October 1945, then No 37 MU at Burtonwood and finally No 38 MU at Llandow. Late in 1951, NS997/G was one 74 FB VIs allocated to the *Jugoslovensko ratno vazduhoplovstyo* (JRV, or Yugoslav Air Force), the Mosquito being flown out to Yugoslavia on 3 April 1952

15
FB VI PZ170/YP-D of No 23 Sqn, Little Snoring, late 1944

Hatfield-built FB VI PZ170 served with Nos 141 and 239 Sqns at West Raynham in mid-1944 before joining No 23 Sqn at Little Snoring, in Norfolk, where it was coded YP-D.

It is fitted with an ASH nose radome containing an AI XV narrow-beam radar for use on low level intruder operations. Flying as part of No 100 Group's Bomber Support force, No 23 Sqn scored its first victory using ASH on 31 December 1944/1 January 1945 when a Ju 88 was shot down over Alhorn by Sqn Ldr J Tweedale and Flt Lt L I Cunningham. PZ170 remained on strength with the unit until August 1945, when No 23 Sqn upgraded to NF XXXs. It was then placed in storage until passed on to the *Armée de l'Air* on 7 October 1946.

16
FB VI PZ459/3P-D of No 515 Sqn, crewed by Plt Off L G Holland and Flt Sgt R Young, Little Snoring, February 1945

Delivered new to 'A' Flight of No 515 Sqn at Little Snoring, where it was coded 3P-D 'D-Dog', this aircraft was flown by Plt Off Leslie George 'Dutch' Holland and Flt Sgt Robert 'Bob' Young (an ex-infantryman from the 'Ox and Bucks', the famous 43rd and 52nd of Foot) on most of their ops in 1944-45. One of these missions included a low-level encounter with a He 219 nightfighter whilst coming back from a Night Intruder patrol to Hailfingen airfield, near Stuttgart, on 14/15 February 1945. Toward the end of the appointed patrol period a contact was detected closing up from behind by the rearward-looking Monica radar. Thus began a desperate 'dance in the dark' where both opposing crews relied entirely on radar to get them into a position whereby they could prevail over their assailant.. For the FB VI crew, they had to rely on the rather limited capability of the AN/APS 4 ASH (essentially an anti-shipping radar), which was up against a dedicated AI system in the shape of the excellent Lichtenstein SN-2. Having just failed to achieve firing range in their opening 'tail chase' of the Mosquito, the 'Owl' crew were now searching for their target as desperately as 'Bob' Young was in the FB VI, but as no further contact was established, both crews went home to fight another day. PZ459 later participated in an attack on Nordholz which resulted in claims for an Me 262 destroyed and two damaged. The Mosquito then passed to No 141 Sqn in the spring of 1945, and remained with the unit until it converted to NF XXXs later that year. PZ459 was then placed in storage, before being sold for scrap in July 1947.

17
FB VI NT137/TH-T *Lady Luck* of No 418 'City of Edmonton' Sqn, crewed by Flt Lt Jack H Phillips DFC, RCAF, and Flg Off Bernard M Job RAFVR, Hartford Bridge, February 1945

NT137 *Lady Luck* was issued new to Canadian-manned No 418 Sqn in the late autumn of 1944 as part of the unit's conversion from NF IIs to FB VIs. Crewed predominantly by Flt Lt Jack H Phillips DFC, RCAF and navigator, Flg Off Bernard M Job, RAFVR during the squadron's brief spell at Hartford Bridge in February 1945, the aircraft accompanied the unit to Coxyde (B71), on the Belgian coast, in March 1945 for the final hectic weeks of the war on the continent. Following No 418 Sqn's disbandment in September 1945, NT137 was passed to No 13 OTU, with whom it suffered a landing accident on 29 May 1946 at

Middleton St George that resulted in its recatagorisation as instructional airframe 5959M.

18

NF XII HK119/VY-S of No 85 Sqn, crewed by Flt Lt J P M Lintott and Plt Off G G Gilling-Lax, West Malling, May 1943

Some 97 incomplete NF IIs were transferred from the Leavesden production line to Marshall's of Cambridge for conversion into NF XIIs between January and June 1943, HK119 being amongst this number. No fewer than 19 NF XIIs were subsequently issued to No 85 Sqn during the first half of 1943, HK119 arriving at the unit's Hunsdon home on 17 April 1943, where it was coded VY-S. On 29/30 May Flt Lt J P M Lintott and Plt Off G G Gilling-Lax used the fighter to down Ju 88S-1 3Z+SZ of I./KG 66 at Isfield, near Lewes in Sussex – this kill represented the first S-1 to be destroyed over the UK. Gilling-Lax had completed a first-class degree at Marlborough and Cambridge, and had been a house master at Stowe, before joining the RAF as a navigator. He and Lintott were subsequently killed shooting down a Do 217 over Kent on 9 July 1943 in another Mosquito. On 22 January 1944 HK119 joined No 307 Sqn, where it was coded EW-D and used to probably destroy a He 177 on 19 February 1944. The veteran night-fighter was still flying with the Polish-manned unit when it was written off in a landing accident at Andreas, on the Isle of Man, on 26 June 1944 – the pilot lost an engine short of the runway, forcing him to undershoot.

19

NF XIII MM469/NG-X of No 604 'County of Middlesex' Sqn, Lille/Vendeville, France, early 1945

The NF XIII was powered by Merlin 21, 23 or 25 engines, had AI Mk VIII radar installed in either a 'thimble' or Universal ('bull') nose and utilised a Universal wing similar to that fitted to the FB VI. The prototype NF XIII flew for the first time in August 1943, and 260 were eventually built. MM469 joined No 151 Sqn fresh from the Leavesden factory on 29 February 1944, and was passed to No 96 Sqn on 29 July 1944, No 29 Sqn on 14 December 1944 and finally to No 604 Sqn in early 1945. Following the disbandment of the 'County of Middlesex' squadron on 18 April 1945, MM469 was issued to No 409 Sqn six days later, from where it was retired to an MU on 7 July 1945 in the wake of the latter unit's disbandment on the first of the month. It was finally SOC on 9 October 1945.

20

NF XIII MM446/RO-Q of No 29 Sqn, Hunsdon, December 1944

As one of the first NF XIIIs delivered to the RAF, MM446 had the early 'thimble' type nose radome associated early-production examples. Delivered to No 27 MU on 30 January 1944 for final fitting out, the aircraft joined No 151 Sqn at Colerne on 22 February 1944, where it was coded RO-Q. The unit was engaged on 'Insteps' and Rangers at the time, and on 20 April squadron OC, Wg Cdr Geoffrey H Goodman, and Flg Off W F Thomas (an ex-policeman), destroyed a W34 north of Biscarosse Lake, followed on 4 May by no fewer than four He 111s shot

down over Dijon again in this aircraft (a feat for which Goodman was awarded the DFC). This took the crew's tally to eight aircraft destroyed in just two months. On 11 August MM446 was transferred to No 96 Sqn at Ford for night anti-Diver patrols off the East Coast, before moving to Odiham on 24 September to continue its war against the V1. When No 96 Sqn disbanded on 12 December 1944 (reforming nine days later equipped with Halifax IIIs), MM446 joined No 29 Sqn at West Malling 48 hours later for Bomber Support duties – hence its black undersurfaces. The fighter served until 27 February 1945, when the squadron converted to the NF XXX. War-weary and fitted with outmoded radar in comparison with the latest night-fighters then entering RAF service, MM446 was passed to Marshall's of Cambridge for the removal of its avionics, before being broken up on 28 May 1945.

21

NF XIII HK500/RA-I of No 410 'Cougar' Sqn, RCAF, crewed by Wt Offs R Jones, RCAF, and Gregory, RCAF, Zeals, July 1944

Delivered to No 218 MU from Leavesden on 20 December 1943, HK500 was one of twenty-one NF XIIIs from this batch of 137 aircraft issued to No 410 Sqn as replacements for their FB VIs. It arrived at Castle Camps on 7 January 1944, and moved with the unit to Hunsdon on 29 April 1944, from where it continued defensive night operations in the lead up to D-Day. A move to Zeals came on 18 June, by which time nightly patrols were being flown over the Normandy Beachhead. During one such sortie on 23/24 June, Wt Offs R Jones and Gregory destroyed a Ju 188 15 miles north-west of the Beachhead. HK500 was itself lost on 10 July 1944 when it overshot the runway on landing at Zeals following the failure of its starboard engine in flight. The aircraft was consumed by fire in the resulting crash.

22

NF XIII HK428/RO-K of No 29 Sqn, flown by Flt Sgt Johnson, West Malling, June 1944

No 29 Sqn began receiving NF XIIIs in place of its FB VIs in October 1943, and it retained these aircraft until February 1945, when it re-equipped with NF XXXs. HK428 was amongst 20+ NF XIIIs delivered to the unit fresh from the factory in the autumn of 1943, the fighter being used on 17/18 June 1944 by Flt Sgt Johnson to down a Ju 88. Badly damaged in action on 22 October 1944, it was returned to de Havilland at Hatfield for extensive repairs, after which the NF XIII was passed to the Central Gunnery School, where it remained until SOC on 16 September 1946.

23

NF XIII HK382/RO-T of No 29 Sqn, Hunsdon, October 1944

Painted in standard Intruder camouflage on upper surfaces and Smooth Night undersides (this scheme had been adopted on 1 October 1942), HK382 was also amongst the batch of new NF XIIIs delivered to No 96 Sqn in the autumn of 1943, arriving at Drem on 30 October. Its frontline life with this unit was to last just 25 days, however, for on 24 November it was damaged in a flying accident that kept it grounded until September of the following year. Cleared fit to fly once again, HK382 was passed to No 29 Sqn on 20 September 1944, where it was coded RO-T. The unit converted to NF XXXs in February 1945, and HK382 was transferred to No 409 Sqn at B51 Lille/Vendeville, although its career with the Canadians was cut short on 16 March 1945 when it inexplicably dived into the ground nine miles west of its home airfield.

24
NF XVII HK286/G/RX-A of No 456 Sqn, RAAF, crewed by unit OC, Wg Cdr K M Hampshire DSO and Flt Lt T Condon, Ford, March 1944
One-hundred NF IIs powered by 1460 hp Merlin 21 or 23 engines were converted to NF XVII specification through the fitment of American SCR·720/729 (AI Mk X) radar – the first of these aircraft took to the skies in March 1943. Amongst those converted was HK286/G, which reached Australian-manned No 456 Sqn on 29 January 1944, where it was coded RX-A and used by unit OC, Wg Cdr Keith MacDermott Hampshire DSO and Flt Lt Tom Condon. The pair experienced great success in this aircraft, starting with two Ju 88s shot down on 27/ 28 February 1944 off the south-west coast. On 24/25 March they destroyed Ju 88 AP+3E of 6./KG 6 over Walberton, in Sussex, and three nights later they downed Ju 88s 3E+FT of 9./KG 6 and B3+BL of 3./KG 54 near Beer and Brewer Isle respectively. On 23/24 April they shot down another Ju 88 into the sea near Swanage, whilst on 28/29 April they probably damaged a Do 217 86 miles off Durrington. On 22/ 23 May they downed a Ju 88S off the Isle of Wight, and on 12/13 June claimed yet another Ju 88 over the Channel. HK286/G was finally passed to No 51 OTU on 4 January 1945 after No 456 Sqn transitioned to NF XXXs, the fighter being used for Mosquito instruction until 1 July 1945, when it was returned to de Havilland for minor maintenance work, before being placed in storage. HK286/G was SOC on 21 June 1947.

25
NF XIII HK425/KP-D *Lonesome Polecat* of No 409 'Nighthawk' Sqn, RCAF, crewed by Flg Offs R H Finlayson and J A Webster, Le Culot, France, 6 October 1944
Built at Leavesden in the second half of 1943 and delivered to No 96 Sqn when the unit converted from Beaufighter VIFs to Mosquito NF XIIIs in October/ November of that same year, HK425 was passed to No 409 Sqn when it also traded in its Beaufighter VIFs for Mosquito NF XIIIs in March 1944. On 6/7 October 1944 Flg Offs R H Finlayson and J A Webster destroyed a Bf 110 in this aircraft, followed on 25/26 November by a Ju 88 claimed by Flg Off R I E Britten and Flt Lt L E Fownes over Rheindahlen. The fighter's final kill came on 18/19 December when Finlayson and Webster destroyed a Ju 88 in this aircraft. Its *Lonesome Polecat* nose art was inspired by a drunken Indian character from a very popular comic strip of the day, Finlayson having added the name to the aircraft and then asked his parents to send him a copy of the comic from Canada for copying. However, before the publication arrived, one of his groundcrew painted the skunk on the nose ahead of the titling, and it was considered to be so well done that Finlayson left it on. Having survived the war HK425 was subsequently SOC on 21 November 1945.

26
NF XIX MM644/VI-V of No 169 Sqn, Great Massingham, January 1945
The NF XIX, which first flew in April 1944, was powered by two Merlin 25s and fitted with AI VIII or X (SCR720 or 729) radar in a 'thimble' or Universal nose similar to that utilised by the NF XIII. MM644 was one of 280 built, being delivered to the RAF from Leavesden on 28 April 1944. It served with No 85 Sqn from 20 May 1944 until passed to No 157 Sqn on 8 December. The fighter then moved to No 169 Sqn on 14 January 1945. Following the disbandment of the latter unit on 10 August 1945, MM644 was sent to No 9 MU ten days later and stored until sold to de Havilland for scrapping on 27 October 1948.

27
NF XXX NT362/HB-S of No 239 Sqn, crewed by Flt Lts A J Holderness and Walter Rowley DFC, West Raynham, February 1945
No 239 Sqn was equipped with NF IIs from January 1944, and FB VIs from August of the same year (one FB VI had actually been issued to the unit as early as 31 December 1943). More than 20 brand new, Leavesden-built, NF XXXs finally arrived at the unit's West Raynham base in January 1945, including NT362. The highlight of the latter aircraft's brief war came on the night of 7/8 February when Flt Lts A J Holderness and Walter Rowley DFC destroyed a Bf 110 over the Ruhr whilst flying NT362. The nightfighter was placed in storage following the disbandment of No 239 Sqn in July 1945, although it returned to the air on 9 September 1948 when it was delivered to the Belgian Air Force as MB-14. Its postwar career was to be brief one, however, for on 7 August 1950 it crashed at Beauvechain air base and was declared a Category 5 write off.

28
NF XXX MT487/ZK-L of No 25 Sqn, Castle Camps, November 1944
MT487 was delivered to No 218 MU on 28 September 1944 and issued to No 25 Sqn at Castle Camps on 6 October 1944 as the squadron replaced its NF XVIIs with NF XXXs. These aircraft were then used for Intruder patrols from December 1944 until 1 February 1945, when Bomber Support operations began. MT487 actually took part in No 25 Sqn's final wartime mission, which took the form of a Night Ranger to German airfields on 25 April 1945. The fighter remained with No 25 Sqn until placed in storage in February 1946, and it was subsequently sold for scrap Marshall's of Cambridge on 11 August 1948.

29
NF XXX MV564/G of the 416th Night Fighter Squadron, Twelfth Air Force, USAAF, Italy, November 1944
The 416th NFS (and the 425th NFS in the Ninth Air Force in England) was forced to operate Mosquitoes because of the late delivery into squadron service of Northrop's awesome P-61A Black Widow (see *Osprey Combat Aircraft 8 -*

P-61 Units of World War 2 for further details). This aircraft was lost in action on 22 April 1945.

30

NF XXX NT283/G/HU-V of No 406 'Lynx' Sqn RCAF, crewed by unit OC, Wg Cdr Russ Bannock DFC and Flt Lt Robert R Bruce DFC, Manston, January 1945
NF XXX NT283/G was delivered to the RAF on 24 November 1944 and passed to No 406 Sqn on 18 December, where it was coded HU-V. Equipped with NF XIIs in April 1944, the unit started night intruding patrols soon after receiving its first Mosquitoes, before reverting to fighter sweeps in support of the impending D-Day landings. One of the first units to receive NF XXXs (in July 1944), No 406 Sqn commenced a nocturnal offensive over German nightfighter bases in the late summer of 1944 that would last until VE-Day. Operating from Manston, in Kent, on 5/6 January 1945, NT283/G, with squadron OC, Wg Cdr Russ Bannock DFC, and Flt Lt Robert R Bruce DFC, at the controls, destroyed a He 111 over Josum airfield. On 4/5 April the same combination destroyed a UEA and damaged an Fw 190 over Delmenhorst airfield. Following the war, NT283 saw service with both No 609 'West Riding' Sqn (from 30 April 1946) and No 616 'South Yorkshire' Sqn (from 11 July 1948 through to 24 April 1949). It was finally scrapped in November 1953.

31

FB VI HR147/TH-Z *HAIRLESS JOE* of No 418 'City of Edmonton' Sqn, RCAF, crewed by Sqn Ldr Russ Bannock DFC and Flg Off Bobbie Bruce DFC, Middle Wallop, 8/44
FB VI HR147 of No 418 Sqn was the regular mount of then Sqn Ldr Russ Bannock DFC and his navigator, Flg Off Bobbie Bruce DFC. Issued to the unit in factory-fresh condition, the fighter was to serve as the 'canvas' for a distinctive piece of nose art, and associated scoreboard, inspired by Bannock, and his exploits. In fact the artwork was applied twice, for HR147 suffered damage to its nose in an operational mishap which saw the caricature, and its background disc, repainted – at this time one of the two rows of eight swastikas was replaced with 19 V1 symbols. HR147 was finally sold for scrap in October 1954.

32

FB VI NS850/TH-M *"Black Rufe"* of No 418 Sqn, RCAF, crewed by Sqn Ldr Robert Allan Kipp and Flt Lt Peter Huletsky, Holmesley South, June 1944
FB VI NS850 was also at No 418 Sqn at much the same time as HR147, and like the latter, it too carried rather stunning artwork – at least by the conservative standards of the RAF. Flown by Sqn Ldr Robert Allan Kipp and Flt Lt Peter Huletsky, this aircraft saw much action – see the front cover artwork caption and page 49 for full details.

FIGURE PLATES

1

Flt Lt Ted Cox, 'A' Flight No 29 Sqn, Ford, February 1944. He is wearing standard RAF officer's Battle Dress over a white turtle-necked sweater (note the whistle attached to his left collar). His life jacket is a standard Mk I, whilst his boots appear to be 1943 Issue. Most Mosquito crewmen chose to wear just steel-tipped shoes in the cockpit rather than boots, as the heat from the twin Merlins quickly drove temperatures up in the cockpit once airborne.

2

Wg Cdr 'Bob' Braham DSO, DFC*, Wing Commander Night Operations 2 Group, 2nd TAF, March 1944. Again in Battle Dress, but with a bright pale blue shirt and black tie worn beneath his tunic, Braham is wearing a German life jacket 'acquired' perhaps from a crewmember from one of his many conquests.

3

Wg Cdr John Cunningham, DSO*, DFC*, OC No 85 Sqn, West Malling, September 1943. Wearing what must have been one of the last pre-war lightweight one-piece cotton twill overalls still in existence by 1943, Cunningham has completed his unique attire with a white silk scarf.

4

Flt Lt Gordon 'Peter' Panitz DFC, RAAF, No 456 Sqn, RAAF, Predannack, June 1943. Denoting his RAAF status, Panitz is wearing the distinctive dark blue Battle Dress and Mk I life jacket. His helmet is a Type C, with a Type G mask attached and Mk IV goggles across the forehead.

5

Flg Off R S 'Dickie' Williams, RAAF, No 456 Sqn, RAAF, Predannack, June 1943, Like Panitz, Williams is wearing dark blue RAAF Battle Dress trousers and a bright pale blue shirt and black tie beneath his Mk I life jacket. Note the holstered .38 cal revolver on his right hip which is attached to a waist belt, and the navigator's almost mandatory canvas map and chart bag.

6

Wg Cdr V J 'Pop' Wheeler, DFC*, MC*, Order of St Stanislaus, OC No 157 Sqn, Bradwell Bay, April 1943. Again standard RAF Battle Dress and a bright pale blue shirt and black tie are worn, but with the addition of 1941 Bomber Command issue gauntlets.

BIBLIOGRAPHY

Bowman, M W . *The Men Who Flew The Mosquito*. PSL, 1995
Bowman, M W and Cushing, Tom. *Confounding the Reich*. PSL,. 1996
Brookes, A J. *Fighter Squadron At War*. Ian Allan, 1980
Howe, Stuart. *The de Havilland Mosquito*. Aston 1992
Mosquito Aircrew Assoc. *The Mossie* Vol 13, April 1996
Mosquito Aircrew Assoc. *The Mossie* Vol 16, April 1997
Sharp C Martin & Bowyer, Michael J F. *Mosquito*. Crecy Books, 1995
Shores, Chris & Williams, Clive. *Aces High*. Grub Street, 1994
Smith, David J. *DH Mosquito Crash Log*. Midland Counties, 1980